Inside the Cockpit

&

the Trading Room

My years as an airline pilot and investment adviser

Lim Kok Kean

with

Pong Pui See

Inside the Cockpit & the Trading Room

Published by:

Pramugari Beauty & Fashion

86, Jalan Tasik Indah 1,
Taman Tasik Indah,
51200 Kuala Lumpur,
Malaysia.

Email: limkokkean.kenanga@gmail.com
IG: howard_limkokkean
FB: Pramugari Beauty & Fashion

References to specific securities and their issues are for illustrative purposes only and are not intended to be, nor should they be interpreted as, recommendations to purchase or sell such securities.

Ordering Information:

Special discounts are available on quantity purchases by corporations, associations, and others. For details, contact the author at the address above.

ISBN: 978-967-18503-0-5

Printed in Kuala Lumpur, Malaysia by:

Percetakan Kenzu
661, Jalan 24,
Taman Perindustrian Ehsan Jaya,
Kepong,
52100 Kuala Lumpur,
Malaysia.

This book is dedicated to my family and friends.

Contents

<u>Preface</u>

I am an airline pilot and investment adviser from Malaysia.

This book was written during the Movement Control Order (MCO), a preventive measure implemented by the federal government of Malaysia to contain and curb the spread of the Covid-19 pandemic in the country. MCO started on the 18th of March 2020.

Throughout my career in the airline, I've had frequent questions on how to become a pilot, the life of a commercial airline pilot, how a plane flies, my view on the frightening MH370 and MH17 incidents and many others. Through these conversations, I noticed that the general public have some misconceptions about flying and the aviation industry, such as junior pilots fly domestic sectors while senior pilots fly internationally. Some even fear flying, thinking of it as a risky activity when truth is, statistics and historical data have shown that driving is far more dangerous, with 250,000 road accidents to every flying accident[1]. Moreover, road accidents result in over 1.17 million deaths each year worldwide[2] and the number is on the rise. Meanwhile, according to ICAO's[3] accident statistics, in the 12-year period from 2008 to 2019, there were less than 4.8 accidents for every million flights, with the lowest accident rate recorded in 2016 at 2.18 accidents for every million departures worldwide[4]. Furthermore, this number is declining as a result of ever-improving aviation technology, enhanced training standards and improved governance of the aviation industry. However, many people may still think that driving is safer because being in the driver's seat makes them feel safer. Moreover, although road accidents occur everyday, their effects are less noticeable, while plane crashes make headlines and therefore grab more attention. As a result, people are more sensitive to them. With these in mind, I decided to write this book to talk about my experience in aviation among other things.

The second part of this book was written by my co-author, Ms. Ceci Pong Pui See. Ms. Ceici was a cabin crew in AirAsia and Singapore Airlines. She currently works for Canadian Aviation Electronics (CAE)[5] as an expert on inflight services. In her section of the book, she talks about her experience working for the world's best low-cost airline, AirAsia[6], and the world's best airline, Singapore Airlines[7].

The final part of this book capitalises on my experience as an investment adviser. Here, I talk about the importance of investing and my investment strategy. I started investing when I was 22 years old and I've learned some valuable lessons the hard way. With this book, I hope my readers will avoid the costly and silly mistakes I made. In Asia, Malaysia in particular, the general consensus is that the best investment one can make is in real estate while stocks are a risky and lousy investment. Is this true? In this part of the book, I explain what risk is and recommend ways to reduce it, all while boosting one's investment returns.

Please enjoy.

Part One

Inside the Cockpit

Chapter 1.

Taking to the Sky

My Road to the Cockpit

I was born in 1987, the year the Dow Jones Industrial Average (DJIA) plummeted 22.6% in a day[8], the largest single-day drop in history. I come from an average family. My father is a businessman. He owns and runs a manufacturing business. My mother works for my father, in his factory, as an accountant. I have a sister and a brother, and I am the eldest son in the family. In traditional Chinese families like the one I was raised in, there is a lot of pressure on the eldest son to thrive, and I try—hopefully with success—to be a good role model. Today, my sister is a licensed lead auditor and holds a master's degree in both psychology and business administration, whereas my brother practices medicine in Melbourne, Australia. I couldn't be prouder of them.

I went to Chong Hwa Independent High School in Kuala Lumpur. It is a private Chinese secondary school that bases its teachings and curriculum on the references and guidelines of Dong Jiao Zong. At the end of my schooling, I earned a Unified Examination Certificate (UEC) that is not recognised by the Malaysian government. However, it is recognised by many universities in Australia, the U.K., the U.S., Japan, Singapore and others. I was also a police cadet as a student. There, I learned discipline, teamwork and leadership. These qualities have greatly aided me in both my life and career. I recall that after class every Saturday, we would undergo intense physical training that was nothing less than the real police training. We would jog 10 kilometres, do 100 push ups, squat jumps, sit-ups, and the like. We would also visit the police station on National Police Day that falls on March 25th.

After graduation, like most students, I had no clue which path to take to further my studies. Since my father runs a manufacturing business, I decided to enrol myself in a business administration course at Help University in Damansara. I thought I would one day follow in the footsteps of my father and become a manufacturer.

But one day, something struck my mind. "I wanna be a pilot," I said. My neighbour, who was a pilot for Singapore Airlines, inspired me. That moment was the turning point of my life. The next day, I quit university and took up an English language class at the British Council, knowing that a good command of the English language is a basic requirement of becoming an airline pilot. Indeed, several studies have shown that human errors account for over 80% of air traffic accidents[9], most of them caused by misunderstandings that resulted from poor communication. One of the worst air traffic disasters occurred in March 1997 when 2 Boeing 747s collided on a runway on a foggy day, taking 583 lives[10].

I spent 6 months improving my English at the British Council. There, I met many friends from different cultures all around the world. I can't overemphasise the importance of a conducive learning environment when picking up a foreign language. Since no one spoke Mandarin in class, I finally got the chance to practice my English. Never was I so eager to learn the language, thanks in no small part to the environment and the atmosphere.

Fear

Many traditional education systems incorporate fear into learning. Students are often told "study hard so you won't fail your exams" or "don't do that or you will be punished". For ages, learning has been driven by fear instead of the desire to acquire new knowledge. Try asking a student why he or she goes to school and spends hours a day in class, and you are likely to get replies like "I have an exam to take", "This is what people my age do" or "If I skip class, I will get expelled".

More often than not, it is fear that holds people back from achieving their wildest dreams. In other words, fear has killed more dreams than the lack of capital, talents, ideas and skills have.

After I matured, I learned that fear is a powerful tool that politicians regularly use. Some politicians establish the perception that if the people don't vote for them, they would lose their privileges.

To quote former U.S. president Franklin D. Roosevelt, "The only thing we have to fear is fear itself".

My Flying School

At the age of 20, I enrolled in a flying school on Langkawi Island. North of Penang Island, Langkawi Island is a beautiful tropical island and popular tourist destination that attracts nearly 3.8 million tourists[11] annually[12]. Just check the number of flights to the island to get a sense of how popular it is. Langkawi is also where the Langkawi International Maritime & Aerospace Exhibition (LIMA)[13] is held bi-annually.

I spent two years at the academy earning my Commercial Pilot's Licence (CPL). The training programme consisted of two major phases: ground training and flight training. Both were equally intense. However, some trainees might find one more intense than the other.

During ground school, I learned subjects that ranged from principles of flight to meteorology, radio navigation and other aviation-related subjects. Initially, I had a hard time coping because I was an arts and business student back in secondary school, and you must possess a good foundation in both maths and physics in order to excel in those ground school subjects. I remember being the only one in class to fail the first paper exam. In order to catch up with my batchmates, I spent weekends and hours after class reading and studying. I am glad my hard work eventually paid off.

As you might have guessed, it is really hard to learn to fly by simply reading books. Just imagine for a moment that you are learning to drive a car but you have never sat in one before; all you have is a manual—visualising would be difficult. Today, we have resources that weren't available to us back in the day. There are countless videos on the internet demonstrating how a plane flies and how to fly one. The advent of the internet has made everyday life simple and convenient, not to mention the creation of new professions such as the YouTuber, which was non-existent decades ago. Therefore, undeniably, flying was a learning process; one that I was determined to ace.

Every morning, we would gather on the parade ground and sing the national anthem, *Negaraku,* before heading to class.

Most of the ground instructors were retired Indian Air Force officers and generals. At first, I expected them to be tough because after all, they were from the air force. But they turned out to not just possess knowledge and experience, but also be generous with that knowledge and combat experiences, not to mention patient when teaching their students. Indeed, they were like generals leading their subordinates (students) through battles (exams) by equipping us with mastery and skills. They inspired us to become not only competent pilots, but also responsible human beings. I am very grateful for their support, guidance and precious life lessons.

After completing ground school, I entered the flight-training phase where I learnt to fly the Diamond 40 and Diamond 42[14]. Some students performed well in ground school but underperformed in flight training, while others were vice versa. If ground school training was the theory exam to earn your driving licence, then flight training was the on-road lessons. The two are interconnected but totally different in practice. If you have a problem in ground school, you could always ask the ground instructor for help or refer to your textbooks. On the other hand, during flight training, you won't have time to open a book when your plane is stalling or spiralling out of control. You are basically on your own, especially when you are flying solo.

My flying school had flight instructors from Denmark, Italy, Pakistan, Hong Kong, Myanmar and Japan. During my first lesson, the Dane instructor demonstrated how to fly straight and level, maintaining altitude and airspeed throughout. Again, as with the initial stage of ground school, I struggled to fly the plane competently. I wasn't assertive enough and was 'waiting for things to happen' instead of 'making things happen'. Landing the plane was difficult, especially in windy conditions. Despite that, my instructors were patient in teaching me and I am very grateful for the help they offered. I remember taking them out to meals in exchange for some extra lessons. After several flight lessons, I eventually mastered flying the little plane.

Ground preparation is of utmost importance. The more thorough the ground preparation, the safer the flight will be. Before each flight, we would carefully inspect the aircraft for any defects and check if the engine oil and fuel quantity was sufficient. On top of that, we checked the current and forecast weather of the airport and intended flight route. Before every cross-country flight, we would plot checkpoints on a navigational map and mark the magnetic headings we were to fly on each leg. In addition, we would note the safe altitude to fly that would allow us to clear the surrounding terrain yet maintain two-way communication with air traffic controllers as well as receive signals from navigational aids.

One day, I operated a solo flight from Langkawi to Penang. Flying along the coastlines of Kedah, I saw spectacular paddy fields, rolling hills, curvy rivers, and lively towns and villages. It was breathtaking. After landing at Penang International Airport, I went into the terminal for lunch before heading back to Langkawi. Watching the big commercial passenger planes taxi in front of me, I swore I would one day pilot one.

During a flight training sortie one day, my instructor and I flew to the northeast of Langkawi, a training area dedicated for student pilot training. It is where we practice flight manoeuvres such as rate-one-turns, steep turns, climbs and descends, etc. Suddenly, the instructor idled the engine power to simulate loss of power. I was completely stunned and my blood went cold as the plane slowly lost both speed and altitude. Despite my initial reaction, the instructor just sat there quietly with his arms folded. Right then, I knew I had to show him my ability to cope with this kind of emergency. I took a deep breath, calmed myself down and thought of the emergency procedures I had learned. I had two options: attempt to relight the engine or, if that was unsuccessful, perform an emergency forced landing on land. Alternatively, I could ditch in the water if my speed, altitude and position rendered solid land too far away. With that in mind, I performed the engine relight procedure, and he gave me my engine back. What a relief! The moral of the story was that being a pilot, as with an investor, I must always have a contingency plan. In case things don't go as desired, there must always be a way out. That is also the reason why as a financial consultant, I always stress the importance of having a steady stream of passive income to my investment clients. Because we don't know when our engine (active income) might fail.

During the later stage of flight training, I flew the Diamond 42, a twin-engine propeller aircraft. Like before, the instructor would occasionally cut one of my engines off. But it was different this time, because I still had one operative engine, and the aircraft was flyable with only one engine running. Nevertheless, due to the sudden yaw that resulted from the loss of an engine while the other ran at high power, I had to kick the rudder to maintain my course. To get a sense of this, just imagine that the left wheels of a car stopped spinning while the right wheels continue to turn at a high speed; the car would swing abruptly to the left and lose control. I remember my legs shaking after those flights.

In 2009, at the age of 22, I graduated from the flying school with a Commercial Pilot's Licence (CPL) and frozen Airline Transport Pilot's Licence (ATPL). At 28, I received my fourth bar and got promoted to the rank of captain.

Chapter 2

Joining the Airline

Shoe Sales Promoter

2009 was a really tough year. That year, the world suffered the aftermath of the 2008 subprime mortgage crisis. Economists call it "The Great Recession". The moniker was coined due to the collapse of mortgage-backed securities and the subsequent credit and liquidity crisis that ensued. The Standard & Poor's 500 index (S&P 500)[15] crashed approximately 50%, bringing the global economy down with it[16]. The U.S. Federal Reserve (U.S. central bank) and the U.S. Department of Treasury responded by slashing interest rates to near zero, bailing out failed systemically important financial institutions and engaging in quantitative easing[17] in an attempt to stimulate the stalling economy. The financial crisis spread globally, and Malaysia was not spared.

The Kuala Lumpur Composite Index (KLCI)[18] tumbled nearly 39%[19]. Thousands of companies went out of business and millions of people lost their jobs. The demand for jobs rose rapidly whilst the supply collapsed. It was a relatively tough year for both businesses and consumers. There was a casual saying that once you graduated, expect to be jobless.

While most businesses were downsizing, cutting costs and laying off staff to survive the economic downturn, one company expanded rapidly despite finding itself in the worst recession since The Great Depression. It was none other than Skytrax's world's best low-cost airline, AirAsia[20].

After graduation, I sent my carefully crafted resumes to both AirAsia and Malaysia Airlines System (MAS), the national carrier of Malaysia. Meanwhile, knowing that it would probably take a long time to land a job in the airlines, I took a part-time job at a shoe shop on Petaling Street[21] as a sales promoter.

Everyday, I met hundreds, if not thousands, of customers and tourists from all over the world. Serving customers and helping them find suitable shoes was particularly tough for me since I was introverted and shy. Once, a lady from Africa visited the shop. She held stacks of cash in her hands and it immediately caught the attention of all the sales promoters in the shop. I plucked up the courage to walk up to her and asked, "Good afternoon, ma'am. How may I help you?"

"I want a pair of each kind of shoe in this shop; every size, but only brand-new pairs." She continued walking around the shop and barely looked at me.

"Sure. A moment please." I ran to my shop manager and told her about this. We were both excited. The next day, the lady sent her assistants to collect the shoes. That sale netted me a handsome commission and the shop a good profit.

I had taken Arabic lessons, harbouring plans to apply for a job at Emirates, the dream airline of many pilots. That helped a lot since many of the customers were from the Middle East. I would speak Arabic to them and simultaneously learned a few Arabic words in return. They were very happy to teach and would tip me before they left. Sometimes, they would even invite me to their home in their country. They were friendly people and I am grateful for the opportunity to meet them.

Job Interview

After 3 short months, I received a letter from AirAsia, inviting me to a job interview and written test. Many of my batchmates waited as long as a year to hear back from the airlines, but I was lucky.

To prepare for the interview, I studied the history of AirAsia, the organisational chart, the current routes, the ins and outs of the aviation industry and everything related to the airline. I was a bit nervous as I had never been to an interview before and didn't know what to expect. However, I knew that it was ultimately a sales process, although in this case, instead of promoting shoes, I was going to promote myself.

That morning, I got up early, had breakfast, put on a coat and took a taxi to AirAsia's headquarters. I arrived there at 7 a.m. and the office was still closed. I wandered around the airport terminal to kill time and observe how the airline business operated. The terminal, Low Cost Carrier Terminal (LCCT), was filled with people. Clearly, it was too small to handle the ever-increasing passenger volume.

At 8:30 a.m., an office assistant led me and several other candidates into the office and gave us a paper test and some forms to fill. I completed the test within an hour. It consisted of basic questions on aerodynamics, maths and physics. After that, we entered a small room one by one for the face-to-face interview. I was the last candidate to go in. Finally, it was my turn.

"Sit down, young man," the interviewer said.

I greeted him politely and obliged.

"Tell me about yourself," he added. After some chit-chat, he began to test my technical knowledge. He asked, "What is MORA? What is MEA?"

The final question he asked was a scenario-based one: "Imagine that you are flying a plane at night and your captain, who has more than 20 years of flying experience, is the pilot flying. You notice that the plane is flying below a safe altitude and there is high terrain ahead, but your captain insists that it is fine. What would you do?"

I thought for a few seconds and replied, "I would take over the controls and execute a climb until a safe altitude is reached."

After a week or two, I got a call from AirAsia inviting me to sign an employment agreement. I joined AirAsia as a second officer and started training in July 2009.

Training

My batchmates and I were sent to AirAsia Academy (now known as AACE) for ground training and classes. We learned many subjects: airline security, threat and error management, crew resource management, safety and emergency procedures, standard operating procedure, company policies, dangerous goods, aircraft systems and others. Parts of the training were conducted with computers, called computer-based training (CBT), a type of e-learning, where we self-studied the operation and systems of the Airbus 320, the plane we were going to pilot.

The next phase was fixed-based simulator (FBS) training, where the system knowledge acquired from CBT training was put to practical use with AirAsia's SOP. The programme was designed to train the crew in normal and abnormal operations through task sharing and crew coordination. The idea was for the crew to master the procedures before training in the full-flight simulator (FFS), because every minute in the FFS cost a lot more. From here, I learned that teamwork is the key to a safe and efficient flight. And that's why airliners require multi-crew operation, so the pilots can keep each other accountable.

In school, teamwork can sometimes be an iffy thing. Teamwork isn't always revered. For example, teamwork during exams is considered cheating and the students will be punished. Do it again and they might get expelled from school. Having said that, I believe that the intrinsic need to be part of something bigger is one of the reasons why students like sports like basketball, baseball, badminton and football; these games allow them to practice teamwork and cooperation. The same can be said for online games where a group of players plan and execute their missions.

The final phase of ground training involved the full-flight simulator. The flight simulator is a machine operated by a hydraulic system that simulates real-life situations. It allows pilots to get comfortable with the controls and aircraft-handling without being on an actual flight. After all, you can't simulate engine fire or rapid decompression on a real aircraft with passengers on board, neither can you learn to ride a bike by merely reading a book. Instead, you must experience the real thing. As *Xunzi*, a Chinese Confucian philosopher, once said, "Tell me and I forget. Teach me and I remember. Involve me and I learn."

Every time before our simulator session, my simulator partner and I would meet up one day before to study the syllabus, the airport charts and discuss the failures we were likely to encounter. Next, we would visualise the scenarios.

Once, before the simulator session in a briefing room, the instructor said, "I want you to make as many mistakes as you can and learn from them. The more mistakes you make here, the less mistakes you will make on the real plane." I wish every instructor thinks like he does. We human beings are designed to learn from mistakes. Just like when you first learned to ride a bicycle. You tried and you fell. You made mistakes, learned from them and got better each time. Eventually, you learned to balance and pedal forward. In a version of the story, Thomas Edison[22] was

26

reported to have been asked during an interview how it felt to fail 1,000 times. His alleged reply was, "I have not failed. I have discovered 1,000 ways not to make a light bulb."

In the flight-full simulator, the instructor would throw all kinds of failures and emergencies at us. If we made mistakes or needed improvement on a particular exercise, he would note it down to discuss with us at the end of the session. Learning in this way was fun. I remember my school days when students were punished for making mistakes. That restricted learning and instilled fear in us, making learning unappealing. As Kelvin Wong, the author of *The Principles of Wealth*, said, "The only people who don't make any mistakes are those who don't do anything."

The final training phase before pilots are cleared for line operation is line training. During line training, student pilots operate revenue flights under the supervision of a flight instructor to familiarise themselves with normal line operations.

For my first line training flight, I flew from Kuala Lumpur to Kota Kinabalu. The day before the flight, I studied the airport charts carefully: the taxi routings; the departure and arrival procedures. Then, I noted all the air traffic control frequencies[23] on a piece of paper. On the day of the flight, I arrived at the flight operations office early to prepare the relevant paperwork. I had the mindset that if my instructor arrived at the office before I did, even if I was there before sign-on time, I was late. At the office, I checked the aircraft status sheet for defects that might lead to performance penalties. I also looked at the forecasted weather of my flight route, destination and alternate airports[24]. Next, I calculated the fuel required for the flight and read through the Notice to Airmen (NOTAM).

Approximately 2 hours before the departure time, the instructor arrived at the office and I promptly walked over to shake his hand and introduce myself. I then briefed him on the flight information. He was impressed. After he signed the flight plan and decided on the amount of fuel to carry, we proceeded to the departure hall with our cabin crew. In the cockpit, he asked, "What training are we undertaking today?"

Without a single thought, I replied, "Line training to become a first officer."

"Wrong," he said. "We don't train you to become a first officer. We train you to be a captain. The moment you put your butt on this seat, you are training to become a captain. Being a first officer is just part of the process. Eventually, you will command this plane on your own."

We took-off from Runway 32R of Kuala Lumpur International Airport, climbed to 37,000 feet, flew eastward over the South China Sea and headed for Kota Kinabalu. During cruise, he explained the reasoning behind the standard operating procedures to me. He didn't just show me how to carry out the procedures, he also explained why the procedures were designed the way they were. "Airbus has consistently collected data from airline operators around the world for decades; researching, designing and redesigning. They studied and investigated accidents and incidents, and didn't let a single one go to waste before they finally came up with this SOP. So, it is important that you understand the reason behind every procedure and action."

It was a beautiful day with clear skies. We landed 10 minutes ahead of the scheduled arrival time. After we completed the actions required by the parking checklist[25], the instructor asked, "Do you know what Kota Kinabalu is famous for?"

"Seafood?" I asked slowly.

"That's right," he replied with a grin. Then, he went into the terminal and bought Seafood Fried Rice for the cabin crew and I. It was the best Seafood Fried Rice I ever tasted. What a nice instructor he was.

After about 2 months of line training, I passed the final line check and was cleared to operate line flights as a junior first officer.

Chapter 3

How to Become a Pilot

Introduction

Piloting an airliner and earning a good salary have always been an enticing proposition for many young secondary school and college graduates. However, unlike other professions, those who wish to pursue the flying path often find little to no information about it at education fairs and college orientation days. After I finished secondary school in 2005, it took me several months to gather information about the steps necessary to become a pilot. Therefore, in this chapter, I include a step-by-step approach on how to become a pilot.

Types of Pilots

When people say "pilot", they generally refer to commercial airline pilots. However, commercial operation isn't the only type of flying there is. They are also charter pilots, air ambulance pilots, flight instructors, government service pilots, law enforcement pilots, military or air force pilots, fire fighter pilots, agricultural pilots, air show stunt pilots, test pilots and even drone pilots. If you want to become a pilot, your next course of action depends on the type of flying you want to do, as different types require different licences. If you want to fly a small aircraft for recreational purposes, a Private Pilot's Licence (PPL) is good enough. If flying a commercial jet and carrying passengers is what you prefer, you will need a Commercial Pilot's Licence (CPL). If you hope to one day become a captain of an airline, fly a commercial aircraft and receive a handsome salary, you will need an Airline Transport Pilot's Licence (ATPL). For the sake of this book, we will focus on only commercial airline pilots in Malaysia.

Medical Licence

Professional airline pilots have to deal with unique and challenging demands in their line of work that could affect their personal wellbeing. To become a commercial airline pilot in Malaysia, you must obtain a Class 1 medical certificate from a specialised aviation medical examiner who is certified by the Civil Aviation Authority of Malaysia (CAAM)[26]. During the medical examination, your general health, blood, urine, hearing, eyesight and heart rate will be examined. The candidate must be free of any congenital and acquired abnormality, any latent, active, acute or chronic disability, and any other health conditions that could jeopardise the safe operation of a flight[27].

It is mandatory for every commercial pilot to undergo a Class 1 medical examination every year. Pilots aged 60 and above are required to undergo medical examination every 6 months[28].

Among the most common in-flight incidents is pilot incapacitation, a state in which the pilot's ability to carry out his or her normal flight duties is severely impaired. The most extreme example of pilot incapacitation is sudden death, which often results from a heart attack. However, this is not necessarily the most hazardous type of incapacitation. Subtle incapacitation, a progressive degradation of a pilot's capability to perform flight duties[29], is more difficult to recognise and is therefore more dangerous.

On the 16th of November 2012, the captain of a flight bound for Abu Dhabi became incapacitated due to a stroke as the aircraft was positioning for approach to land. The first officer took over the controls and declared the emergency to the air traffic controller. The first officer then landed at the airport uneventfully. The investigation revealed that the captain had an undiagnosed medical condition which predisposed him towards the formation of blood clots in his arteries[30].

It is therefore vital that pilots maintain good physical and mental health at all times.

English Language Proficiency Test

Flawless communication is of paramount importance to the safety of air travel. English is the official language of the civil aviation world. The International Civil Aviation Organisation (ICAO) has made it a requirement that every pilot and air traffic controller sit for a test conducted by an authorised English language examiner before they are allowed to operate.

The test aims to measure the candidate's English language proficiency in aviation-related environments, listening and speaking skills, and the ability to comprehend aviation radiotelephony messages and respond to them using ICAO aviation terminology. The candidate is assessed in the following 6 areas: pronunciation, fluency, structure, vocabulary, comprehension and interaction. The candidate will be graded on a scale between 1 to 6. The lowest score determines the final English proficiency level, and the candidate must score level 4 or higher to pass the test[31].

One of the world's deadliest mid-air collisions occurred on the 2nd of November 1996 over a small village west of New Delhi, India, when two passenger aircraft collided, killing 349 people in total[32]. The investigation found that a lack of proficiency in the English language was the major contributor to the fatal air crash.

International air travel has played an important role in globalisation by fostering the movement of goods and people. The pilots' good command of English is one of various ways to maintain that.

The Flying Schools in Malaysia

Commercial flying schools focus on training professional pilots. There are numerous flight schools that provide the same training programmes but differ in fees and quality. As of the year 2020, a pilot training course typically costs around RM 350,000 (81,400 USD). Since that is a lot of money, it is a good idea to shop around before deciding on the flying academy that best suits your needs. It is also a good idea to consult pilots from various flying academies to learn about their training experiences.

The following are flying schools registered with the Civil Aviation Authority of Malaysia (CAAM):

1. Malaysian Flying Academy (MFA) in Melaka.

2. HM Aerospace (HMA) on Langkawi Island.
3. Layang-Layang Helicopter Academy (LLHA) in Kota Kinabalu.
4. International Aero Training Academy (IATAC) in Melaka.
5. Helang Flying Academy (HFA) in Johor.
6. Asia Aeronautical Training Academy (AATT) in Johor.

More detailed and updated information can be found at www.caam.gov.my.

Requirements

The requirements to enrol in a pilot training programme may vary from academy to academy, but they should not differ too much from the guidelines set by CAAM. They may include (in Malaysia)[33]:

1. Minimum age of 17 years old.
2. Holds a *Sijil Pelajaran Malaysia* (SPM) certificate with a minimum of 5 credits which include English, mathematics and science, or other equivalent or higher educational certificates.
3. A letter of approval from CAAM.
4. Pass a Medical Class 1 examination carried out by a CAAM-approved aviation medical examiner.

5. Pass an entry test and interview.

Ground School

Ground training consists of 950 hours that typically take about 8 to 12 months to complete. It is divided into several phases and includes the following subjects[34]:

1. Principles of flight
2. Human performance and limitations
3. VFR and IFR communications
4. Aircraft general
5. Meteorology
6. Instrumentation
7. Radio navigation
8. General navigation
9. Mass and balance
10. Type technical
11. Aircraft performance
12. Flight planning
13. Air law
14. Operational procedures
15. Airframe
16. Electrics
17. Power plant

18. Radiotelephony

The student must score 75% or above to pass the examinations. The difficulty level resembles those of tertiary- or diploma-level examinations.

Flight Training

A student pilot is required to complete 135 hours of flight training on a single-engine aircraft, 30 hours in a single-engine flight simulator, 25 hours in a twin-engine aircraft, and 10 hours in a twin-engine flight simulator[35]. He or she must complete a minimum of 200 flying hours to earn a Commercial Pilot's Licence. Candidates are required to demonstrate competency in both Visual Flight Rules (VFR) flying[36] and Instrument Flight Rules (IFR) flying[37]. It is crucial that pilots develop good IFR skills so that they can fly even if the weather is bad or visibility is limiting. All of AirAsia's flights are conducted under IFR rules.

In the initial stages of flight training, the student, under the supervision of a flight training instructor, will practice his or her flying in Visual Meteorological Conditions (VMC) by using outside references and a navigational map. During this stage of flight training, the main focus will be on mastering the four fundamentals of flying: climbs, descents, turns, and straight and level flying. After several flights, the student should be skillful enough to handle the aircraft without assistance and be cleared for his or her first solo flight[38].

During the subsequent stages of flight training, the student will practice flying in Instrument Meteorology Conditions (IMC) by wearing a view-limiting device that allows him or her to see only the instruments in the cockpit. The student would then fly based on the references and signals of the navigational aids, the way airline pilots usually fly.

During the final stages of flight training, the student will fly a twin-engine light aircraft. This part of the training focuses on the handling of different abnormal and emergency conditions such as engine failure.

At the end of each flight training phase, a test will be conducted and the student must demonstrate his or her ability to operate the flight safely and efficiently.

What distinguishes a competent and skilful pilot from the rest is the training he or she has undergone. Consider this: According to the International Transport Forum, Germany has one of the lowest road accident fatality rates in the world. Between 2000 and 2018, the number of road accident fatalities even fell by 56%[39]. That was significant progress. This is in a small part due to the excellent driving training that each licence applicant must undergo before earning their driving licence. A German driving licence costs around 2,000 USD, requires a minimum of 45 hours of professional instruction and 12 hours of theory lessons[40]. The theory test itself is difficult as one-third of the candidates fail the test. That says a lot about how seriously the Germans take driving. This is also an indication that if other nations desire to bring down their road accident fatality rates, reforming and restructuring the driving courses is the way to go. Likewise, the strength of a pilot's training would determine his or her abilities.

After meeting the necessary requirements, a student pilot would earn a Commercial Pilot's Licence (CPL) with a frozen Airline Transport Pilot's Licence (ATPL), and the candidate is ready to apply for a job with an airline.

Cadet Pilot Programme

A flying course typically costs over RM 350,000 (84,000 USD) in Malaysia. That is a lot of money. For many people, the largest hurdle to becoming a pilot is affordability. Fortunately, many major airlines have their own cadet pilot programme. This is an amazing opportunity for fresh graduates to pursue their career in aviation. The candidate will be guaranteed employment by the airline upon successful completion of the flying course. For this reason, I recommend that anyone who wishes to become an airline pilot attempt to get into an airline's cadet pilot programme.

Since the financial cost of training a pilot is substantial, it is natural for airlines to seek the best of candidates to join their team of professional pilots. The minimum requirements vary from airline to airline, but they generally include (in Malaysia)[41]:

1. Malaysian citizen.
2. Age between 18 and 28 years old at the time of application.
3. Minimum height of 158cm.
4. Good command of English and Bahasa Malaysia, both written and spoken.
5. Physically fit.
6. Distant visual acuity with or without visual correction shall be 6/9 or better in each eye separately, and binocular visual acuity shall be 6/6 or better. Refractive error shall not exceed 5 diopters.
7. Academic qualifications:
    a. Sijil Pelajaran Malaysia (SPM) or equivalent with grade A in mathematics and English, grade B in physics or grade A in general science, and grade B in any other two subjects.
    b. Diploma or degree prerequisites:
        i. Engineering or scientific-related discipline.

ii. CGPA of 3.0 and above.

iii. SPM with a grade B in any five subjects, of which must include English, mathematics and science.

Applicants who fulfil the above requirements will then be required to undergo several assessments. This includes:

1. Psychomotor test - A test that assesses the multitasking capabilities, reaction, coordination, control, precision and dexterity of the candidate.
2. Psychometric test - Also known as aptitude test, it evaluates the candidate's cognitive ability and personality.
3. Panel interview - It is a data collection process where the interviewers communicate directly with the candidates to determine if they are suitable for the job.

Successful candidates will be shortlisted and those eventually selected by the airline would be enrolled into the airline's Multi-Crew Pilot's Licence (MPL) programme to earn a Multi-Crew Pilot's Licence (MPL) with a frozen Airline Transport Pilot's Licence (ATPL). Alternatively, they might earn a Commercial Pilot's Licence (CPL) with a frozen Airline Transport Pilot's Licence (ATPL)[42]. Upon completion of the training, the cadets will fly with the airline as junior first officers.

Some of the cadet pilot programmes are self-funded. Successful candidates may apply for a loan from the airline's partner bank to finance their training.

Discipline

Contrary to popular belief, being a pilot, as with a financial investor, requires more self-discipline than intelligence. It means having self-control, following standard operating procedures (SOPs), respecting limitations, abiding by flight rules and regulations, rejecting opportunities for shortcuts, and others. For example, some airlines require their pilots to avoid alcohol 10 hours before a flight duty and it takes more self-discipline than intelligence to adhere to this rule. Human errors account for more than 80% of aviation accidents and the major contributor is the failure of pilots to follow SOPs[43]. Lack of discipline is the root cause of these deviations and therefore a major threat to flight safety.

Similarly, many gamblers blame gambling and casinos for their distress and devastating financial situations. But the root cause of their suffering stems from poor self-discipline, not gambling or casinos. They simply

42

yielded to temptations and did not control themselves. Likewise, the reason why so many people fail to lose weight is because they lack self-discipline. Instead, they resort to weight loss supplements (shortcuts) to achieve their desired bodyweight and get instant gratification, often at the expense of long-term health.

Self-discipline is very important for pilots.

Chapter 4

Inside the Cockpit

Pilot Ranks

The airline pilot uniform was first introduced by Pan American World Airways[44], a former international carrier of the U.S. that was founded in 1927[45], and was inspired by naval officers. Ranking stripes on the epaulets make the uniform complete. However, different airlines use different colours. Have you ever wondered what those epaulets and stripes on a pilot's shoulders mean? They indicate the pilot's rank and level of experience. In AirAsia where I launched my career, the second officer (a student pilot under training) wears one bar on each shoulder. The junior first officers wear 2 bars. Meanwhile, the senior first officers wear 3 bars, whereas the captains wear 4 bars.

Epaulets may be of any colour. AirAsia, for example, uses platinum colour while Malaysia Airlines System (MAS) issue gold-coloured apulets.

Pilot Salary

Flying a big jet and carrying hundreds of passengers to their destinations is a glamorous and rewarding career, both financially and spiritually. Global air-traffic passenger demand has been growing significantly over the past three decades and is expected to accelerate due to the emergence of the middle class around the world. This, combined with a worldwide shortage of pilots, has led to an increase in pilot salaries. Basically, a pilot's salary is made up of three components: flying allowance, basic salary and sector allowance. Pilots don't earn a flat monthly salary like other professionals. Instead, they are paid for hours flown, also known as flying allowance or productivity allowance. However, many airlines do pay their pilots guaranteed flying hours, so that even if a pilot were to fly below that minimum amount, he or she can count on at least a minimum amount of salary every month. Nonetheless, the monthly basic salary is fixed but incremental, increasing in proportion to the number of years of service in the airline. Meanwhile, sector allowance is the salary paid for each sector the pilot operates.

Pilot salaries also vary from airline to airline and the type of aircraft flown. Regional and low-cost airlines generally pay less than major airlines and flag carriers. In the past, regional airlines were regarded as stepping stones for pilots on their way to a major airline. But to cope with pilot shortage, many regional airlines have revised their pay scales to more competitive and generous amounts.

Pilots of non-jet aircraft (propeller aircraft) typically make significantly less than pilots of jet aircraft because jet aircraft generally carry more passengers and cargos.

Generally, in Malaysia, a junior first officer of a commercial jet starts out with a monthly salary of RM 8,000 (1,860 USD). In comparison, the senior first officer earns RM 20,000 to RM 30,000 (4,650 USD to 7,000 USD) while the captain makes RM 40,000 to RM 60,000 (9,300 USD to 4,000 USD).

Before the Covid-19 pandemic, China was a major reason behind the world's pilot shortage[46]. Due to its growing middle class, more and more people could afford to fly. It was reported that planes were sitting on the ground due to pilot shortage. In an attempt to attract foreign pilots, some airlines in China offered very attractive and generous remuneration packages, including pay cheques of over 300,000 USD a year, tax free[47]. Moreover, to compete with the other local airlines in the country, some airlines even offered a loyalty bonus of 40,000 USD if the pilot remained in the airline for 3 years.

The European Commission projected that by 2030, over 70% of China's population would be middle class, consuming nearly 10 trillion USD in goods and services. They have also predicted that India would become home to the world's largest middle-class consumer market, surpassing both China and the United States[48]. In addition, other emerging economies in Southeast Asia, such as Cambodia, Myanmar and Vietnam, achieved average economic growth rates of more than 6.8% in 2019[49]. That is nearly 3 times greater than the growth rate achieved by the United States and nearly 10 times greater than that of Germany and Japan[50]. In the years ahead, more people are expected to join the middle class and this could translate into a huge demand for air travel and by extension, pilots. Economics 101 dictates that when there is growing demand but limited supply, prices will increase. It is no wonder that pilots have enjoyed one of the best pay increments for the past 10 years.

Pilot's Responsibilities

The pilot's job is much more than just flying the plane. Steering the plane and performing take-offs and landings are just a small part of what pilots do. Modern commercial airliners are equipped with advanced and complex automation systems that now handle many routine flight maneuvers that were once performed by pilots. A pilot, especially the captain, is now essentially a manager.

A senior pilot who has achieved the rank of captain would be the pilot in command (PIC) of a flight. The captain is responsible for the overall safety of the crew, passengers, cargos and aircraft. He or she has the final authority in relation to the aircraft and flight operation. Before the flight, the captain (or delegated member of the crew) performs a thorough and careful external walkaround inspection to determine if the aircraft is safe for flight operation before deciding to accept it[51]. The captain is also responsible for ensuring that the crew comply with the airline's SOP during all phases of flight. During pre-flight preparation, the captain, along with the co-pilot, checks the weather forecasts of the destination airport, alternate airports, and the planned flight route, then decides on the fuel quantity to uplift. On top of the forecast weather, other factors that the captain takes into consideration when deciding on the fuel are the facilities of the airport and the aircraft's performance penalty. Next, the flight crew ensures that the aircraft's mass and balance is within limitations, then ensures that the licences, passports and other documents of the crew are valid and up to date. The PIC should always lead by example, encourage teamwork, motivate the crew, engender a good working atmosphere and most importantly, establish a climate for open communication. It is crucial that the captain be open-minded, listen to his or her crew and respect their opinions.

The first officer, or co-pilot, is the captain's deputy. The co-pilot is the second-in-command. If the captain becomes incapacitated, the co-pilot will take over the controls, assume the responsibilities of the captain for the rest of the flight, and land at the nearest suitable airport. He or she carries out all the flight duties that the captain has assigned or delegated, calculates take-off data, checks the flight plans, and supports the captain in achieving a safe flight. The first officer is encouraged to speak up when any doubt arises and be assertive enough to challenge the captain when necessary.

What It Takes to Become a Captain

Becoming a pilot is one thing and becoming a captain is quite another. On average, a pilot takes six to seven years to climb the ladder and ultimately become a captain of a narrow body aircraft [52]. However, several factors play into this. In AirAsia, for example, some take as little as 4 years to become a captain. This is due to AirAsia's low-cost business model that leads to pilots clocking more flying hours and sectors than the average pilot in the industry. The main determinant, nevertheless, is the individual.

A typical airline requirement to become a captain is to clock 5,000 hours and hold a full ATPL. Some airlines like AirAsia require their captains to be at least 26 years old[53]. Meeting the required hours is only the beginning of the process. The airline will then look at the candidate's training and safety records, as well as the candidate's performance before putting him or her through command assessment. Command assessment consists of a command development course, command assessment mentoring flights and a command interview. Upon successfully passing the assessments, the candidate will undergo intensive simulator and line training in which the trainee will assume the role of a captain under the supervision of an instructor. A final line check is the final hurdle before a candidate earns his or her fourth bar. In certain airlines, the candidate will also be required to pass a command evaluation simulator check.

Having said that, other factors also play an important role in promotion. Airlines that aren't expanding or are downsizing usually have a limited number of vacant captain positions and pilots are promoted on the basis of seniority. Therefore, it may take longer to get a promotion in such an airline than ones that are undergoing rapid expansion. In regard to this, low-cost carriers with spectacular growth usually present more opportunities for promotion.

Flight Duty

Unlike nine-to-five jobs, pilots don't have a fixed work schedule. In most airlines, before the end of every month, pilots receive a published flight roster that lists the individual's flight duties for the subsequent month. According to regulations, pilots are only allowed to fly a maximum of 900 hours in every 12-month period[54] and that works out to 75 hours a month[55]. The roster also includes a couple of standby duties during which the pilot is not rostered to fly but must be prepared to go for flight if called to do so. Standby call-ups usually happen if someone falls sick or is unable to undertake the flight duty due to unforeseen circumstances. Sometimes, it is for legality reasons that result from bad delays. Every crew has a limited flight duty period, and delays might put them at risk of busting this limitation.

Airports and airlines get a lot busier during holiday seasons. Families and vacationers depend on airlines to get them to their holiday destinations and home. Therefore, it is part and parcel of a pilot's job to miss holidays, birthdays, anniversaries, weekends and parties. In

Malaysia, pilots do not get paid extra for working on holidays.

Pre-Flight Preparation and Briefing

The general public thinks that pilots start work when they enter the cockpit, but in reality, the job starts long before the flight. Like passengers, pilots generally arrive at the airport several hours before departure time. As mentioned in a previous paragraph, both the captain and first officer will check the validity of each other's licence, passport and other documents as flying with an invalid document is illegal and punishable by law. They will then analyse the technical status of the aircraft they are going to operate, look through the operational flight plans (OFP), weather forecast reports, various charts[56], Notice to Airmen (NOTAM)[57] and SNOWTAM[58], if any. In an airline, these are usually prepared by the flight dispatchers. This is the planning stage during which the pilots determine the amount of fuel required for the flight after taking all the above into account. For example, if the weather forecast indicates a heavy storm along the flight route, the captain might carry extra fuel to cater for weather deviation or possible airport congestion that may result from flight delays and holdings[59]. If the NOTAM reports the unserviceability of a navigational aid at the destination airport, the pilots will discuss the issue and develop an alternative plan, since airline pilots always fly with navigational aids, and the lack of one might present a problem.

Pre-flight briefings are vital so that every crew member is aware of their role in the flight. The pilots and cabin crew meet to discuss the flight details and all aspects of the flight such as the expected weather en route, special local procedures imposed by the airport authority, VIPs on board etc, before making their way to the aircraft. Any foreseeable issues are usually clarified at this stage.

Aircraft Exterior Inspection

A thorough exterior walk around to inspect the aircraft's physical condition is the next step of pre-flight preparation. The pilot visually checks for obstruction of the probes and ports; checks the vents for leaks[60]; checks for brake wear and condition of the tyres; checks for contamination of the critical flight control surfaces[61]; checks for the presence of foreign objects that might damage the aircraft; checks the condition of the engines and cowlings. The pilot also ensures that all ground activities[62] are carried out according to the SOPs in a safe manner.

On the 2nd of October 1996, a Boeing 757 took off from Miami International Airport with the static ports still covered by tapes. Immediately, the pilots noticed that their instruments were showing erroneous readings of both the airspeed and altitude. Since the flight was operated at night without visual references, neither the pilots nor the air traffic controllers knew the actual altitude the aircraft was flying at. Faced with a lack of reliable instruments, the airspeed reduced so drastically that they experienced multiple stalls before crashing into water inverted, killing all 70 crew and passengers on board[63].

A careful exterior inspection could have prevented the disaster and saved 70 lives.

Cockpit Preparation

Cockpit preparation is carried out in anticipation for take-off. It starts with a review of the aircraft technical and maintenance logs [64] to ensure that the aircraft is safe and legal for operation. The pilots will then start up and programme the aircraft's Flight Management and Guidance System (FMGS)[65] before the initiation of passenger boarding. This is done with a checklist so that no important steps are missed. The cabin crew would carry out their own tasks in the cabin to ensure that all the emergency equipment is serviceable. Any defects are reported to the captain or engineer immediately. It is important to note that the seat belt sign is turned off during refuelling to enable rapid evacuation should an emergency arise. In the cockpit, the pilots would obtain the relevant weather information and calculate the take-off weight and speeds[66]. They will then request for departure clearance from the air traffic controller via radio. Next, both pilots will cross check the setup and perform a briefing[67]. The briefing is critical because it makes certain that both pilots share a common vision for the flight, especially if an emergency were to happen during take-off.

After the passengers board, aircraft is refuelled and the departure clearance is received, the aircraft will be ready for pushback and engine start.

Take-Off

When the pilots receive taxi clearance, they would taxi the aircraft to the runway for take-off. Before take-off, they use the checklist again to confirm that the aircraft is correctly configured and ready for take-off.

On the 26th of December 1968, a Boeing 707 cargo flight bound for Vietnam crashed during take-off in Tokyo, Japan, killing all 3 crew members on board. Investigators later discovered that the take-off was performed with the flaps in the retracted position and an aural warning system that was designed to alert the pilots did not activate[68]. It was concluded that the main cause of the catastrophe was the failure to use the cockpit checklist.

Upon receiving take-off clearance, the pilots will complete the checklist and confirm that the aircraft has entered the correct runway before setting take-off thrust.

Take-off is a critical phase of flight. Therefore, if a failure occurs during this time, the captain will seriously consider aborting the take-off if there is sufficient runway length to stop the aircraft. Decision speed, or V1, is a predetermined speed designed to aid the pilots in making this critical decision. V1 is defined as the speed beyond which the take-off should be continued even if an emergency, say, engine failure, occurs, because aborting the take-off would lead to a runway overrun that could result in severe aircraft damage. Beyond V1, even if the engine has failed, the aircraft is capable of getting airborne safely and climbing at a gradient that would allow obstacle clearance.

The cabin crew will always instruct the passengers to turn off their mobile phones and electronic devices before take-off and landing. According to aviation regulations, the use of portable electronic devices, which emits electromagnetic radiation, is not permitted below 10,000 feet even in flight mode. It is important that passengers observe the rules to avoid potentially dangerous interference that could affect the electronic and avionics systems in the cockpit, inadvertently jeopardising the safety of the flight.

In 2003, a plane crashed short of the runway at Christchurch Airport, killing all 8 people on board[69]. Investigators later discovered that the pilot had called home during the flight and the call remained connected, which might have interfered with the aircraft's navigation system.

Typical take-off speeds for single-aisle passenger jetliners are in the range of 260 to 280 kilometres per hour. The heavier the aircraft, the greater the speed needed for lift off. During the take-off run, as the speed increases, lift generated by the wings overcomes the aircraft's weight and flight is achieved.

Climb

After take-off, the aircraft will climb to a cruising level that allows it to clear all terrain and obstacles. Contrary to popular belief, an aircraft depends on the excess thrust of the aircraft's engines to climb and not the lift generated by the wings. That is why a rocket can climb without wings. During initial climb, the pilots will retract the slats and flaps that were used during the take-off[70].

Above 10,000 feet, if the weather is favourable, the pilots may turn off the seat belt sign so that the cabin crew can commence the service of in-flight meals and beverages.

Cruise

Upon reaching the desired cruising altitude, the pilots level off. They then fly at an airspeed that suits their goals of fuel-efficiency or time-efficiency, depending on their preference. The typical cruising speed of a jetliner is approximately 800 – 900 kilometres an hour. Usually, aircraft cruise at higher altitudes on long distance flights and at lower altitudes for short distance flights[71].

Whilst the pilot's workload during cruise is not as heavy as it is during take-off and landing, contrary to popular belief, pilots don't just sit there and talk about sports while the autopilot does all the work. Every 30 minutes, the pilots perform a fuel and time check to determine if the rate of fuel consumption differs from the planned rate. This is also when pilots with good airmanship constantly ask the "what if" questions: What if the engines fail now? What if a fuel leak develops? What if a passenger gets ill and needs immediate medical assistance? What if the hydraulic system malfunctions? Where is the nearest suitable airport in case an emergency occurs and a diversion is necessary? Are the facilities at the alternate airports sufficient to support our operation? The pilots would establish contingency plans in case an emergency arises and a diversion is necessary.

One of the primary reasons why aircraft fly at high altitudes is that air gets thinner as the aircraft climbs. Thinner air reduces drag which translates into less resistance, which results in more air miles covered per unit of fuel. This is similar to a person walking on solid land as opposed to in the water. Besides, aircraft are able to avoid most weather when flying at high altitudes since most weather phenomena occur at low and middle altitudes. Another reason for flying at high altitudes is for emergency reasons. If the aircraft suddenly loses power in all its engines, the pilots would have a higher chance of gliding safely to an airport if they started at a higher altitude.

On the 24th of August 2001, Air Transat Flight 236 bound for Lisbon lost both engines while flying at 39,000 feet over the Atlantic Ocean due to a fuel leak. Without power, the pilots proceeded to glide the Airbus 330. They glided for 19 minutes and covered 75 miles before eventually landing at Lajes Air Base. All 306 people including the crew survived[72].

Approximately 80 nautical miles before top of descent, the pilots would obtain the destination and alternate airports' weather information. They will then prepare the Flight Management and Guidance System (FMGS) for arrival and calculate the landing performance[73], taking into consideration the wind speed and direction, temperature, atmospheric pressure and runway surface condition. Next, they carry out an approach briefing. When they are ready, the captain might make a public announcement to inform the passengers of the weather at the destination and the estimated time of arrival.

Descent

During the descent phase, the aircraft leaves its cruising altitude for approach and landing. Throughout this phase, the pilots would constantly perform mental calculations in order to determine if the aircraft is on the descent profile. As a simple example, if the remaining distance to landing is 100 nautical miles, the aircraft should be at around 30,000 feet and at the correct speed. If the aircraft is flying at 35,000 feet, it is "too high", and prompt actions are necessary to regain profile. If, on the other hand, the aircraft is flying at 25,000 feet, it is "too low", which would mean reduced terrain clearance and higher fuel consumption.

Different airspaces have different standards and procedures. For example, countries like China, Russia, Mongolia and North Korea use metres as the unit for height, whereas Malaysia, Singapore and other nations use feet. As a consequence, it is essential that pilots are properly aware of the airspace procedures.

Approach and Landing

Approach and landing—the final phases of a flight—is when the pilots bring the aircraft back to the ground. To slow the aircraft down, the pilots extend the slats and flaps as they position the aircraft for final approach to land. During the last moments of flight, the pilots reduce the rate of descent just before the aircraft touches down on the runway by executing a gentle flare to induce a smooth landing. Upon touchdown, the pilots deploy the reversers and spoilers to decelerate the aircraft and bring it to a stop.

Approach and landing are highly complicated flight phases. They account for over 56% of all air traffic accidents and 44% of fatalities worldwide[74]. The combination of high workload, close proximity to the ground and increased potential for unanticipated circumstances are likely reasons for this record. In sharp contrast, these flight phases typically consume less than 16% of the total flight time[75]. In an attempt to reduce the risk during these critical flight phases, many procedures and training programmes have been developed to assist the pilots in flying a safe approach and landing. The most prominent is the stabilised approach criteria where the aircraft must be at the recommended speed, attitude, and flight path while fully configured with the checklist completed before reaching 1,000 feet. In case any of the requirements are not fulfilled, a go-around or missed approach must be executed.

Go-Around or Missed Approach

When, for any reason, the pilots perceive the approach to be unsafe and they cannot continue without risking the safety of the flight, they will perform a go-around or missed approach. A go-around or missed approach is similar to a take-off in a sense, except it happens at the end of an approach. Very often, it is unexpected and stressful. During a go-around, the pilot will apply full thrust, change the aircraft's configuration and start climbing. They will then follow the missed approach procedures whilst complying with the performance and regulatory requirements of the airport chart. When they are able, the pilots will inform ATC of their actions and complete the checklist. After some preparation, the pilot will be ready for a second approach to land. However, the pilots might opt to divert to an alternate airport if they deem this the most prudent course of action. During initial training, pilots are often taught: "If unsure, go around! If in doubt, go around!"

Autoland

When the visibility of the airfield has deteriorated to the extent that a visual landing is impossible[76], pilots may perform an autoland using the aircraft's automatic landing system, subject to airport facilities. It is most commonly used during winter when heavy mist, fog or snow is present. However, it can also be used at any level of visibility and when deemed fit by the pilot, such as when he or she feels tired after a long flight. Performing an autoland requires the close coordination of both the pilots and each of them must first undergo special training and certification.

Situational Awareness

In layman terms, situational awareness means always knowing where you are, where you are going, what is happening and what is likely to happen next. For a pilot, it means having an understanding of the current state and environment, the position of other traffic and being able to anticipate any possible threats that might arise in the future. In aviation, we call it "being ahead of the aircraft." Situational awareness can be enhanced by better knowledge, experience, automation, effective communication and teamwork.

Loss of situational awareness has contributed to more air traffic accidents and incidents than all aircraft technical failures combined. There are many factors that could cause the loss of situational awareness: stress, fatigue, distractions, high workload and emotions.

On 31st July 1992, Thai Airways Flight 311 crashed into a mountainside 37 kilometres north of Kathmandu, Nepal, killing all 113 people on board. Upon investigation, it was revealed that the captain, faced with a technical failure, poor weather conditions, frustrating and misleading communications with the ATC, had suffered an emotional breakdown and subsequently lost all his situational awareness. Seconds before impact, he ignored the warning of his co-pilot that the aircraft was flying into a mountain. This was despite the Ground Proximity Warning System (GPWS)[77] sounding continuously[78].

In order to improve flight safety, airlines around the world have developed various guidelines to assist pilots in enhancing their situational awareness. They include:

1. *I'M SAFE checklist[79]*.

- Before every flight, the pilot will ask whether:

(**I**) Is he or she suffering from any illness?

(**M**) Any medication is being taken?

(**S**) Is he or she under mental or psychological stress?

(**A**) Alcohol consumed?

(**F**) Is he or she fatigued?

(**E**) Has he or she eaten enough?

2. ***C.L.E.A.R. concept*[80].**

- This is often used in the decision making process.

(**C**) Calm down, confirm and clarify the problem.

(**L**) Look for options and ideas.

(**E**) Evaluate the different solutions.

(**A**) Act on the decision.

(**R**) Review the performance.

3. ***Threat and error management*[81].**

- It is used as a safety analysis tool to identify a threat and develop a solution to it or establish effective measures to prevent a threat from developing.

4. *Verbalise, verify, monitor*[82].

- **Verbalise**: Speak up when a problem is present to encourage open discussion.

- **Verify**: Adhere to SOP and verify all the changes that had been made.

- **Monitor**: Crosscheck and keep track of the changes that had been made. Modify them if necessary.

Aviation Security

Safety and security are of paramount importance and are the top priorities of the airline industry. Aviation security refers to the measures taken to safeguard passengers, crew and aircraft. Those measures include screening of passengers, crew members and their baggage. X-ray scanners and metal detectors have been installed at all regulated airports to aid the screening process.

With passenger volume growing annually, the airline industry faces increasingly challenging security threats. Airports and aircraft have become potential targets for terrorism and other forms of unlawful interferences. Following the infamous September 11 attacks where two hijacked commercial airliners crashed into the World Trade

Centre in Lower Manhattan, one crashed into the Pentagon, and another crashed into a field in Stonycreek Township in Pennsylvania[8384], many safety and security measures have since been introduced. The cockpit door has since been made bulletproof and access to the cockpit must be authorised. Passengers are prohibited from entering the cockpit during flight. In some major airlines, air marshals are placed on board to improve security and deal with unruly passengers. In addition to X-ray machines and metal detectors, full-body scanners, hand-held detectors and millimetre-wave machines are also used at major airports to check for hidden weapons and explosive items.

On the 21st of December 1988, Pan Am Flight 103, a scheduled transatlantic flight from Frankfurt to Detroit, exploded mid-air, killing all 259 people on board and 11 people on the ground. Investigators found fragments of a circuit board and a timer and concluded that a bomb, not technical failure, had caused the explosion[85].

Technology and digitisation have brought great improvements and conveniences to our lives but at the same time placed the airline industry under ever-increasing threats of cyberattacks. Once, the check-in system of a major busy international airport was hacked, causing massive flight delays[86]. Tens of thousands of passengers were affected. It took the airport IT team 12 hours to restore the system and get everything back in order.

To promote aviation safety and enhance security awareness, airline crewmembers are required to attend a Security Management System (SMS) course and pass a paper test every year. The training course includes the following topics: introduction to Security Management System (SMS), management commitment, threat and risk management, accountability and responsibilities, resources, assessment and reporting, and incident response[87].

Pilots and cabin crew may be the last line of defence in preventing aviation disasters, but security is everyone's responsibility!

Chapter 5.

<u>Misconceptions about Flying</u>

Commercial air travel has become increasingly popular and commonplace, and it is now breeding ground for myths and misunderstandings, often due to inaccurate and sensationalised reports by the media. Hollywood's unrealistic aircraft scenes, too, have contributed to the misconceptions. Throughout my 12-year career in AirAsia, I have been frequently asked questions about air travel and the aviation industry. Through these conversations, I noticed that the general public have certain misconceptions about flying and much of what they think is incorrect. This chapter is therefore devoted to busting these myths.

Misconception 1: Junior pilots fly domestic routes, whereas senior pilots fly international routes.

As far as the airline industry is concerned, there is no such restriction. Junior pilots, like senior pilots, though less experienced, are well-trained and have gone through a series of rigorous training and intensive tests before they were released by the flight training department for line operations. They are armed with the needed knowledge and skills to deal with emergencies should one arise.

The junior pilot, usually a co-pilot in the cockpit, is the second-in-command. Both the captain and co-pilot have their share of flying duties. As with the captain, the junior pilot is also capable of flying the aircraft. In case the captain becomes incapacitated or is unable to continue the flight duties for health reasons, the co-pilot will take over the controls and assume the responsibilities of the captain. The co-pilot is equipped to safely bring the plane and passengers back to the ground.

Moreover, if an airline were to really establish restrictions where the junior pilots fly domestic routes while senior pilots fly international ones, its operating costs will increase substantially as the airlines would have to hire more pilots. Not only will it make air travel more costly, it will also render operational planning less flexible.

Having said that, there are some differences between domestic and international flights. International flights require the crew to clear immigration and go through the screening process at customs. In addition, as different countries have different air laws, pilots must be fully informed to abide by the rules of the respective airspaces.

Misconception 2: Transit is the time when pilots and cabin crew take a break.

Far from true. In fact, transit is when the pilots and cabin crew are busiest with various pre-flight duties to prepare the aircraft for their next departure. Most short-haul flights are multi-sector duties where the aircraft either returns to its original airport or flies on to another one.

Among a pilot's many transit duties are: exterior inspection or walkaround, reporting any defects (if found) to the engineer, carrying out the cockpit security-check, programming the Flight Management and Guidance System (FMGS), collecting weather information, determining uplifted fuel, calculating aircraft operating weights and take-off speeds, reviewing the airport charts, analysing potential risks and threats, conducting emergency and departure briefings, and requesting for departure clearance from ATC. In other words, it's a lot like the preflight preparation mentioned in the previous chapter, and there is a lot to do.

In the cabin, the cabin crew will clean the cabin and lavatories, tidy up the passenger seats, receive and prepare the deliveries from the in-flight catering service staff, perform cabin security and emergency equipment checks, report any defects to the captain or engineer (if found), welcome boarding passengers, direct passengers to their respective seats, assist passengers in storing their hand-carry baggage in the overhead compartment (although this is not their job), remain vigilant for suspicious items, brief the passengers seated next to the overwing emergency exits, advise passengers to switch off their electronic devices, ensure passengers have fastened their seat belts, that tray tables are stowed and seats are in an upright position, conduct passenger departure safety briefing, and report to the pilots when the cabin is ready for take-off. As you can see, transit is a busy time for the cabin crew too.

In AirAsia, all these are completed within 25 minutes, making it one of the most efficient airlines in the world.

***Misconception 3: Cabin lights are dimmed or turned off for take-off and landing to calm nervous passengers and first-time flyers.**￼*

Have you ever wondered why the cabin lights are dimmed or turned off during take-off and landing[88]? If you think it has something to do with safety, you are heading in the right direction.

Every procedure in the cabin is established on the basis of safety. Cabin lights are dimmed or turned off during take-off and landing for your eyes to adjust to the brightness or darkness outside the aircraft. The human eyes take time to adapt to their surrounding brightness and this may slow down evacuation if an emergency occurs that requires the passengers to disembark or deplane quickly. However, passengers are allowed to use the overhead light if they wish to read.

During night flights, however, cabin lights are sometimes dimmed or turned off so that the passengers can sleep.

Misconception 4: Window shades are raised during take-off and landing to give passengers a better view.

Again, it is about safety. Window blinds are raised during take-off and landing, in addition to allowing your eyes adjust to the light outside the aircraft, it also helps the cabin crew see outside better so they can access any potential danger outside the aircraft in case an emergency evacuation becomes necessary.

According to international aviation safety standards, an emergency evacuation must be completed within 90 seconds[89]. A closed window shade, a reclined seat, a poorly stowed tray; any of these might jeopardise and slow down the evacuation, and might result in casualties.

Nevertheless, there are other factors that might lead to slow emergency evacuation. On the 5th of May 2019, Aeroflot Flight 1492, a scheduled commercial flight bound for Murmansk, Russia, suffered an electrical failure caused by lightning strike during the initial climb out. The pilots returned to the departure airport for an emergency landing. The aircraft made a hard landing, causing the undercarriage to collapse. Fuel consequently spilled out from the wings and a fire erupted. As a result, an emergency evacuation was carried out from the forward cabin doors. During the evacuation, many passengers insisted on taking their hand-carry luggage off the burning plane, which slowed down the evacuation process and blocked the exits. The tragedy claimed 41 out of 78 lives. Investigative reports indicate that some of those lives might have been saved if the passengers didn't regard their hand-carry luggage above the lives of other passengers[90].

Misconception 5: If you are born on board a flight, you get to fly for free for the rest of your life.

This is a myth in its purest form. There is no such agreement between passengers and airlines regarding birth on board. In AirAsia, expectant mothers who are 35 weeks and above pregnant are not permitted for carriage[91]. Meanwhile, many other airlines don't carry women who are more than 36 weeks into their pregnancies[92].

But although it is rare, it does happen. According to an unofficial number, 60 babies have been born on board since the beginning of commercial air travel[93]. In case a baby is born on board, cabin crew, who are well-trained in first aid, are there to offer assistance. If that happens, the pilots will likely initiate an emergency diversion to the nearest suitable airport for medical assistance.

Misconception 6: Long-haul flights are more challenging than short-haul flights.

It is general consensus that a 4-hour flight, say, from Kuala Lumpur to Hong Kong, demands more skills out of a pilot than a 20-minute flight from, well, Penang to Langkawi for the simple reason that the flight time is longer. However, the opposite is true. Given that the workload on both the flights are roughly the same[94], the pace of operation is a lot faster for short-haul flights, where decision-making, preparation and planning have to be completed quickly.

From a pilot's perspective, long-haul operations constitute a better lifestyle. If a pilot clocks an average of 75 hours a month, he or she will report for work maybe only once a week. On top of that, long-haul pilots usually operate one sector a day and generally get more days off per month. However, there is a drawback with long-haul operations. Long-haul pilots might become rusty in skills and struggle with jet lag. They operate an average of 6 to 8 sectors a month, giving them less practice on take-offs and landings. In sharp contrast, a short-haul pilot may operate as many as 6 sectors a day!

Misconception 7: Small planes are less safe than big airliners.

We live in a world where size matters. A big motor vehicle is generally believed to be safer and more powerful than its smaller counterparts. However, this is not a fair assumption, because what really matters is the skills and experience of the pilot rather than the size of the aircraft. For example, an Airbus 330 is not necessarily safer than an Airbus 320.

According to the World Health Organisation (WHO), approximately 1.35 million people die each year from road traffic accidents. The top 3 contributors of road accident fatalities are (1) speeding, (2) driving under the influence of alcohol and (3) non-use of helmets, seat belts and child restraints[95]. Road accidents caused by technical failures are rare, irrespective of the size of the vehicle. As with driving, air traffic accidents resulting from technical failures are also scarce.

In a nutshell, the size of an aircraft has no direct correlation to flight safety[96]

Misconception 8: Toilet waste is dumped or jettisoned during flight

We have all heard of this absurd rumour that aircraft dump toilet waste mid-air. The reality is that on modern aircraft, when you flush, the waste that is sucked out of the toilet bowl is collected in a sealed storage container (waste tank), which then gets emptied only on the ground by maintenance staff. The only thing that is dumped mid-flight is water from the sinks.

Misconception 9: If you flush while sitting on the toilet bowl, you might get sucked out.

Aircraft toilets are operated by a closed vacuum system that sucks anything that is in it and stores it in a waste tank. However, the suction isn't powerful enough to suck you in. It is designed and engineered in such a way that you cannot be sucked into it. So, the next time you poop in the aircraft lavatory, don't worry.

Misconception 10: The cabin door can be opened mid-flight.

We have all heard stories of passengers trying to open the cabin door, mistaking it for the toilet door. The fact is cabin doors can't be opened mid-flight due to differential pressures, which is the difference between the pressure inside and outside the aircraft. At 30,000 feet, for instance, the air outside is so thin that its pressure is dangerously low. Meanwhile, the cabin is pressurised to maintain sufficient oxygen for passenger breathing. When the cabin door is closed, the pressure exerted on it from the inside is roughly 8 pounds per square inch[97]. Therefore, it would require superhuman strength to open the cabin door mid-flight.

Misconception 11: Cabin air is unhygienic and full of germs.

Everyone is scared of contracting the Covid-19 virus during flight amidst this pandemic. Contrary to the popular belief that cabin air is full of germs that make you sick, actually, it is relatively clean. Aircraft manufacturers take cabin air quality very seriously and most commercial airliners are equipped with High Efficiency Particulate Arrestors (HEPA), which works continually to recirculate and filter the cabin air. The system also eliminates up to

99.97% of bacteria, viruses, dusts, airborne contaminants and even odour particles in the air. In fact, the air in the cabin is refreshed every 3 minutes to ensure that passengers breathe the highest possible quality of air throughout the flight[98]. This means that the air in the cabin is probably cleaner than the air in your office building.

Misconception 12: Lightning can take down your aircraft.

By an unofficial estimate, every aircraft is struck by lightning more than once a year[99], especially when flying through heavy thunderstorms or a cumulonimbus cloud. Nevertheless, modern commercial airliners are equipped with weather radars that help pilots avoid potentially dangerous weather such as heavy rain and thunderstorms. Pilots are trained to avoid heavy buildups by at least 20 nautical miles. While a lightning strike may be very distressing to the passengers, it is extremely rare that it threatens flight safety, thanks to static dischargers or lightning wicks that are installed on the trailing edges of the wings and tails which dissipates the electrical current into the air.

However, sudden lightning flashes may cause the pilots to be momentarily blinded, especially at night. Hence, there is a procedure that requires pilots to turn on the cockpit lights to full brightness whenever flying in or near a storm cloud.

Misconception 13: Aircraft manufacturers missed row 13 when making planes.

In some cultures, certain numbers carry negative connotations. In the Chinese culture, for example, the number 4 is pronounced as "si", which means death. Therefore, property developers often replace "4" with "3A" on building floors and house numbering.

On board an aircraft, you will have a hard time finding row 13 for the same reason because the number is considered unlucky in many countries and many passengers are reluctant to sit there. Likewise, in some airlines in China, there is no row 4; in Brazil, there is no row 17.

Misconception 14: The probability of you surviving a plane crash is near zero.

Despite being the safest means of transportation, it is reported that over 70% of people still fear flying[100]. According to the analysis by the U.S. Census Data, the odds of dying in a plane crash as a passenger is 1 in 205,552[101]. Now compare that to the odds of dying as a cyclist: 1 in 4,050 and that of a car crash: 1 in 102[102]. MIT Professor Arnold Barnett sums it up best: "A person would have to fly on average of once a day everyday for 22,000 years before they would die in a U.S. commercial airplane accident."

Even if you are unfortunate enough to be involved in a plane crash, there is a 95.7% chance that you will walk out alive[103]. That's due to incredible technological advancements in aircraft systems and rigorous training that pilots must undergo before they are qualified to pilot a plane. In addition, the whole system of air travel, including airports and airspaces, is carefully regulated to ensure the highest level of safety.

Misconception 15: Weather is the most common cause for flight delays.

Adverse weather conditions are often considered to be the main reason for flight delays. However, they are not as common as most people think. Significant meteorology conditions such as typhoons, heavy downpours, snow and tornadoes don't occur frequently and only account for roughly 5% of all flight delays[104].

Air traffic has increased substantially since the 1980s and air traffic control (ATC) has become a very important part of the aviation system. According to the 2019 Aviation

Benefits Report, there were 4.3 billion air passengers in 2018 alone, a 6.4% increase from 2017[105]. However, most air traffic is concentrated in a handful of major hubs such as London Heathrow, Dubai International, Singapore Changi, Hong Kong International and New York's JFK International Airport. Hong Kong Area Control Centre, for example, assumes control of 7 international and regional airports, including Hong Kong International Airport and Macau International Airport. Moreover, aircraft that intend to enter Guangzhou or Zhuhai airspace from the south and east must enter through Hong Kong airspace, making it one of the busiest airspaces in the world. As a means to control and regulate air traffic, many busy and congested airports have imposed traffic restrictions to limit the number of flights entering the airspace for every length of time. Flights departing from Kuala Lumpur to Hong Kong, for instance, are sometimes required to maintain a 10-minute separation.

Another less discussed but more common reason for flight delays is the no-show of passengers at departure time. This might be due to immigration or documentation issues, such as an invalid visa or expired passport; these passengers are denied boarding by the immigration officers after checking in their luggage. To adhere to the on-time departure requirement, ground staff, who assist in passenger boarding, would activate the International Civil

Aviation Organisation's (ICAO) Annex 17 procedure, a security measure designed to prevent any act of unlawful interference against civil aviation, 10 minutes before the scheduled departure time to search for and offload the no-show passenger's baggage[106]. The whole process of identifying, searching and offloading a no-show passenger's baggage is not only time consuming and often results in flight delays, it also increases the operating costs of the airline, since aircraft are like machines—they don't make a profit sitting on the ground.

Misconception 16: The most common emergency encountered by pilots is mechanical failure.

Modern commercial airliners are highly advanced machines and are made up of hundreds of complex systems. Most aircraft systems have multiple redundancies. It means that in the event of a system failure, a standby system will take over and perform the relevant function. This duplication of vital aircraft systems aims to reduce the probability of an in-flight emergency that could result from the malfunction of a major system that could jeopardise flight safety. For example, there is an Auxiliary Power Unit (APU) in every commercial airliner that supplements or takes over if the engine bleed system fails. It also acts as a back-up electrical generator in case the main generators malfunction.

With that being said, in my 12-year career as a pilot, the most common emergency that I have experienced is in-flight medical emergencies.

During a flight bound for Kuala Lumpur in 2019, a male passenger was suffering from epilepsy mid-flight. The cabin crew immediately informed me about the situation and performed first aid on the passenger. The flight was about 30 minutes to arrival time in Kuala Lumpur. After analysing the situation, collecting weather information from all the nearest airports and discerning the time it would take for the medical team to transport the passenger from the airport to the nearest hospital, my first officer and I concluded that Kuala Lumpur was the best option. We then declared our emergency to the air traffic controller, requested for medical assistance and told the cabin crew to prepare the cabin for an earlier landing time. The air traffic controller promptly facilitated our arrival and radar vectored[107] us for final approach to land. The supposedly 30 minutes of remaining flight time was cut down to just 15 minutes. After landing, we were assigned the nearest parking bay for disembarkation. While taxiing in, the medical team which consisted of several paramedics and nurses were already waiting for us at the gate. After parking, they entered the cabin to administer first aid and transfer the passenger into an ambulance.

Dealing with medical emergencies, as with any other emergency, requires the close coordination of the pilots, cabin crew, air traffic controllers and airport management.

Misconception 17: You can judge a pilot's skills by his/her landing.

Most passengers weigh the skills of a pilot by how smooth his or her landings are. If you are a frequent flyer, chances are that you have experienced "hard" and smooth landings before. Despite this common misconception, the success of a landing isn't dependent on how smooth the touch down is. A landing actually depends on many external factors, such as crosswinds, runway length, runway conditions, etc. Even the most experienced of pilots occasionally perform a "hard" landing. Sometimes, the pilot intentionally makes a firm touch down for safety reasons. For example, on a short runway, the pilots will try to touch down as soon as the aircraft reaches the runway threshold. When this is done, they purposely neglect the excessive flaring that is necessary to touch down smoothly because that technique inadvertently eats up more runway length. Similarly, a pilot might perform a positive touch down when landing on a wet runway to break through the layers of water on the runway and prevent hydroplaning[108]. Therefore, a smooth landing is not necessarily a safe landing.

Thus, a landing is no reflection of the pilot's skill and experience. In aviation, safety is always our number one priority, and comfort comes second.

Assuming is Dangerous

I realised that people assume a lot. They often assume that what happened in the recent past will happen again in the immediate future. They also presume that what is right for a particular individual, organisation, company or country would be right for others of the same kind.

A couple of years ago, a friend of mine who is from Hong Kong was on holiday in Malaysia for the first time. She asked me what the exchange rate of HKD to MYR was. I told her that one HKD was worth about 50 cents in Ringgit. She thought it was a joke and assumed that since Malaysia was behind Hong Kong economically, the Ringgit should be less valuable than the Hong Kong dollar.

In 2009, after I successfully joined AirAsia, I asked my friend where the world's 5-star airlines were from. Without hesitation, he replied that they were either from Europe or North America. He assumed that the best airlines were from the developed world. But the actual fact is that they are all in Asia and the Middle East: Asiana Airlines (Korea), Cathay Pacific Airways (Hong Kong), Qatar Airways (Qatar), Singapore Airlines (Singapore), Kingfisher Airlines (India) and Malaysia Airlines (Malaysia).

When Covid-19 initially broke out, many assumed that the developed world would handle the pandemic more efficiently than the developing countries. Again, they were dead wrong.

Assuming is invariably ignorant and dangerous. Without proper analysis and research, assuming that things will happen one way is both foolish and mindless, and can lead to disaster in extreme cases. In aviation, assuming without cross-checking and verifying is known to have caused many accidents and incidents. Perhaps, we ought to learn from the old Russian proverb: "Trust, but verify".

Part 2

Inside the Cabin

by Pong Pui See

Chapter 1.

<u>Shine and Soar</u>

Dream vs Reality

My dream was to become a doctor.

I was once my parents' little princess. Just like any other family, my parents tried their best to give my sister and I the best life they could afford. However, God had a better plan for my dad. When I was 12 years old, he left this world before I could say goodbye. Since then, my family have been without our pillar. I lost the opportunity to learn from the man I love—I'll never love another man the way I love him. At that age, I had to learn to be independent and deal with the loss. Yes, it was a long and lonely journey, but I had promised my dad that no matter how hard life might get, I will always love and protect our family, just like he did. My family struggled financially, so I made the hard decision to enter the workforce right after secondary school, instead of pursuing my dream as a doctor.

I was lucky enough to receive an offer from the Mandarin Oriental Hotel Kuala Lumpur as a purchasing agent, beating many other candidates for the job. Of course, I had my doubts as I had zero experience and zero relevant qualifications. However, my manager assured me that I was capable enough. She hired me, she said, not because of my qualifications, but because she admired how I gave a helping hand to a staff member right before my interview. Working there was a journey, and to this day, I am glad and grateful that my seniors were always there to patiently help and guide me.

Be Humble; Be Kind

Spread your wings and paint the skies RED.

After a year and a half with Mandarin Oriental, I was pretty confident in my role as a purchasing agent. One day, my colleague—who was also a close friend from my department—informed me that AirAsia was hiring flight attendants. I wasn't really into the conversation and started making excuses to avoid the interview. Despite that, she encouraged and prepared me for it. That was the very first time I heard about AirAsia.

AirAsia is a low cost airline that specialises in the ASEAN region. It began with 2 planes and 5 destinations[109]. Within only eight years of operations, the AirAsia Group (including its Thai and Indonesian affiliates) grew to a fleet of 90 aircraft and flew to more than 60 destinations from hubs in Malaysia, Thailand and Indonesia. In 2009, AirAsia operated more than 3,500 flights a week[110]. That year, the group employed close to 7,500 staff and in its short history, had ferried more than 90 million guests [111]. One of the success factors of AirAsia was their people. The company has adopted an ideology where employees are regarded as family, known fondly as "Allstars". AirAsia aspires for their people to feel special and unique, as each of them would play an important role in the company.

On Saturday, as usual, I got on a train and began my journey from Rawang to KLCC. My colleagues and I worked alternative Saturdays. The interview was to be held at the Renaissance Hotel in Kuala Lumpur and my friend convinced me that all would be fine. She promised to be with me until the end of the interview. I had doubts again; I wasn't well prepared at all.

It was a busy Saturday. I got off work at 1pm and quickly got myself ready. My friend and I rushed to the interview venue and were able to complete my registration before 3pm. This was the first round of the interviews where I was required to submit a complete set of my documents.

There were a set of requirements that the candidates were required to meet: ladies must be of a minimum height of 157 cm whereas gentlemen must be at least 170 cm. The measurements were taken while the candidate was barefooted. Subject to changes and airline operator's requirements, the documents required for application of cabin crew position are as follows[112]:

- Original & copy of *Sijil Pelajaran Malaysia* (SPM) with credit in English or any substitute credentials, pass or C in Bahasa Malaysia and a credit in one other subject
- Original and copy of identification card
- Updated/ recent resume and current profile picture
- Original and copy of certificates of higher educations or equivalent

Application was open to all Malaysians 18 years old and above. There were nearly thousands of candidates. Most of them were well-prepared and came with full make-up, hair nicely done and proper attires. I was one of the last few candidates to be called into the interview room. First, they asked me to talk about my favourite food. After my 1 minute presentation on my favourite food, *Nasi Lemak*, I was instructed to proceed to the next interview room. There, the candidates were split into a few groups and we were assigned some activities. The airline was looking for team players who are positive, outgoing and love to be of service to others. I tried my best to perform.

After that, a staff member told me to proceed to the next round where two management staff interviewed me. This was the part when they learned more about us. First impressions are very important so I remembered to keep smiling even though I felt nervous. After completing 4 rounds of the interview process, I was invited for a second day of interview at the then AirAsia Academy in Sepang (this was the old interview process. The current one is completed within a day). My friend, who was accompanying me, was so excited as she prayed that I would succeed in the final interview.

One week later, I showed up at AirAsia Academy for the interview. This time around, I was more prepared with full make-up and a complete set of office attire. First, we were gathered in a room and were separated into a few groups. Each group was given a topic and we had to react to the scenario given to us. After successfully completing the tasks, I was told to proceed for a"skin check". Good looks are important but good grooming is essential to become a cabin crew. For example, braces are not allowed and you must have no visible marks, including tattoos, on your hands and legs. You must have flawless skin with no

94

acne scars and of course, the SMILE! I was one of the lucky candidates who were shortlisted for the final round—the panel interview. I would always remember the moment the interviewers asked me why I chose AirAsia as my first airline. I replied, "AirAsia is the fastest growing airline in the region and I need to earn a lot of money for my family". I know I did not necessarily answer the question. But as I was trying to perform under pressure, I just kept smiling.

AirAsia called me two months later to undergo a complete medical assessment. Upon successful completion of the medical test, I was told, I would be offered a two-year employment contract. An AirAsia employee briefed me on all the terms and conditions in detail. The contract was to be signed and submitted on the first day of training.

And yes, that was how I began my career as a flight attendant, operating on the Airbus 320.

Blood, Sweat and Tears

AirAsia Cabin Crew is an iconic brand. From the red uniform to the warm and bright smiles. Fun and friendly are the ethos of AirAsia Cabin Crew. Although the airline tries to promote a fun culture, do not be deceived for the key duties of the crew include giving instructions during emergencies, calming tensed situations, and enforcing rules and regulations. **WE TAKE SAFETY SERIOUSLY**.

Subject to change, to be an AirAsia cabin crew, you must complete 2 months worth of training. Here are the courses I underwent during my initial training:

- Company Orientation Program[113]
- Computer Based Training[114]
- Image Training
- Customer Service Experience Training
- Communication Programme and Announcement Training
- Aviation Terminology Training[115]
- First Aid Training[116]
- Safety Emergency Procedure Training[117]
- Dangerous Goods Regulations
- Crew Resource Management and Aviation Security Awareness
- HATDP[118]
- Disability Equality Training[119]
- In-flight Services Training
- Flight Time Limitation Training[120]

The safety training in AirAsia is very intensive. There, the priority is always **SAFETY, SAFETY and SAFETY**.

Besides training, crew are required to sit and pass all the exams mandated by the company and the Civil Aviation Authority of Malaysia (CAAM).

We were separated into three batches on the first day of training. Each batch comprised 15 to 20 trainees. There, I met friends from different backgrounds. We shared joy and tears. Serving coffee or tea turned out to be harder than I thought. We also had to carry a heavy manual and lots of loose notes every day, not to mention study hard to pass all the exams. Failure to do so might mean dropping a batch or risking termination. During those 2 months of training, we learned and achieved as a family. 2009 was a very meaningful year for me as I experienced my first ever graduation ceremony. We successfully completed the training and we were ready to pin our wings and paint the sky red. I remember the moment when my boss, Tan Sri Dr. Anthony Francis Fernandes, invited my mum onstage as I received an award—Best Safety Trainee. I teared up. *I made you proud, daddy!*

Even though we were qualified cabin crew then, the training didn't end there. In order to operate solo as a crew[121], all newbies are required to fly a minimum of three supernumerary flights under the observation of a senior cabin crew. Come this stage, we had to apply all the theories that we had learned in class to our work station. My first supernumerary flight in AirAsia was also my first time flying in an airplane! I will always remember my first take-off in the "red bird[122]". On top of that, there was a six-month probation period, and the most important criteria to passing the probation period was discipline—complying with the airline's SOP. Besides that, humility is also essential to success. Be humble and always do your best with a kind and sincere heart. That is my advice to all aspiring crew.

After one year of flying, I was rostered to train for the Airbus 330. AirAsia flies the Airbus 320, a narrow-body aircraft, whereas AirAsia X flies the Airbus 330, a wide-body aircraft. Back then, it was part of the progression to go from narrow-body aircraft to wide-body aircraft.

AirAsia X is the medium- and long-haul wing of the AirAsia Group[123]. AirAsia X launched its first route from Kuala Lumpur to Gold Coast in November 2007[124]. As part of the transition, the crew were required to sit and pass the relevant exams. Although Airbus 320 and Airbus 330 come from the same Airbus family, the safety and in-flight services procedures are quite different.

AirAsia offered me a permanent employment contract two years later. Apart from being eligible for full employee benefits, my salary scheme also increased. A cabin crew's basic pay is around RM 1,000 (240 USD) before tax deduction and increases according to years of service. On top of the basic, cabin crew are paid hourly and sector allowances. Therefore, the total salary a cabin crew will receive at the end of the month depends on the sectors and flying hours of that month. The more you fly, the more you earn!

Because of AirAsia's aggressive expansion, promotions came faster than the average airline. Other than receiving my permanent employment contract, I was also promoted to become a senior cabin crew (SCC) on the Airbus 320. To qualify as a SCC, we had to successfully pass an exam and interview. In addition to that, essential training was provided by the company in order to equip us with effective management skills and develop our leadership qualities. The responsibilities of a SCC are very different from a regular cabin crew, as you are the person in charge of the overall safety and comfort of your crew and passengers. At the age of 22, apart from learning how to become a good leader, I had the challenge of managing people who had more experience than I did. I learned to be more humble and gracious, proactively sharing my intentions while being clear about my vision for the flight. I also learned to be kind, understanding and last but not least, practice strict compliance to the company's SOP. The year I got my promotion, I was so proud to see my younger sister join me in painting the skies red; she became an AirAsia cabin crew.

Goodbye, My Beloved Family

I grew and learned so much with AirAsia, and I never planned to leave this company I regarded as family. However, my commitments were increasing rapidly as I always dreamt of a better life for my family. After serious consideration, I decided to interview for another airline. Apart from the salary, I also wanted to learn and experience different types of flight operations. Leaving was painful and my heart was in pieces although I didn't show it. I sincerely hoped that I would come back one day with all that I had learned and experienced. I yearned for the day when I could contribute and work for my beloved company again.

Goodbye, AirAsia.

Be Brave and Accept Changes

The Blue Uniform.

Singapore Airlines—Singapore's flag carrier—is well known for its multiple travel awards and impeccable service standards. Their kebaya-clad cabin crew, famously known as the Singapore Girl, embody the Singapore Airlines spirit.

The Singapore Girl—branding of Singapore Airline—has been widely successful and is commonly featured in most of the airline's advertisements and publications. To date, Singapore Airline has been ranked the world's best international airline for 25 consecutive years[125].

Becoming an SIA Cabin Crew is a dream to many. Nothing is more awesome than having a job that pays you to travel around the world! If you aspire to apply for this position, please ensure that you meet the minimum requirements. They are, subject to change and also the airline's operator requirements, as listed below (for Malaysians)[126]:

- Minimum age of 18 years old
- Minimum 1.58 m for female/minimum 1.65 m for male

- Degree/Diploma *OR* at least 2 principal level passes and 2 subsidiary passes in STPM/GCE 'A' level or its equivalent *OR* at least 5 credits in SPM/GCE 'O' level and relevant working experience (For Malaysian qualifications at SPM level, at least 5 credits including a minimum grade of B4 in English and working experience is required)

Additionally, you are required to download and complete the application form, as well as bring the following documents for the interview[127]:

- Completed application form
- Passport size photograph
- Originals and copies of birth certificate, passport, identification card and all educational certificates[128]

In 2013, I decided to attend an interview with Singapore Airlines to gauge my own standard. I took an early flight and flew down to Singapore for their walk-in interview. With the flying experience that I had then, I felt more confident, unlike my previous interview with AirAsia. However, my confidence level dropped the moment I entered the lobby of Concorde Hotel in Singapore. There were thousands of candidates applying for the same position as I was. I quickly walked through the crowd and joined the queue in front of the registration desk. Most of the candidates were well-dressed and fully groomed to the standard of Singapore Airlines. After submitting all my relevant documents, I was summoned for a height check. Even though I had listed my weight and height on my application form, I was still required to prove that I could reach the line on the wall barefooted.

Then, I was given a number and told to wait in a huge ballroom. I still remember a few videos playing on a loop in the ballroom and I was amazed by all of Singapore Airlines' destinations. I wished to experience and explore those places, just like the girls in the video did.

A girl was seated to my right and we started a light conversation while waiting to be called. My confidence depleted when I learned that this was her seventh interview with Singapore Airlines. I truly respected her determination. I was glad to hear about her interview experiences, so that I had a better idea of what to expect.

Around half an hour later, ten of us were called into a meeting room. There were two interviewers in the room. We were asked to introduce ourselves and talk about our favourite cartoon character. Our body language and the way we spoke would reflect our confidence level. Should you find yourself in an experience like this, no matter how nervous you get, again, always remember to flash your brightest smile!

Out of the 10 candidates, only two of us were shortlisted for the next round—a male candidate and I. He was a young and outspoken Malaysian guy. Like me, he also travelled to Singapore early that morning, except he came from Johor Bahru—the capital of Johor and a Malaysian town that sits just across the border from Singapore. Similar to the girl, this interview was his ninth attempt for the position at Singapore Airlines and I had a great time speaking to him. I hope he has achieved his dream of becoming a cabin crew with Singapore Airlines.

During the next stage of the interview, we were divided into groups of six. We were given one minute to get to know the candidate next to us. We then had to introduce our partner, such as their background, age, hobby and so forth, to the two interviewers. I was the only candidate from my group of six to proceed to the subsequent round of the interview.

There were only six of us remaining at this point. We were divided into two groups and given a debate topic: We should have another casino in Singapore. Then, we were given two minutes for a quick discussion. My team took the negative stance and each of us had a chance to speak and debate.

Around 2pm on Saturday, I learned that I was shortlisted. I was invited to attend the second interview on the following day, which would be held at the SIA Training

Centre (STC). Unlike the crowd on Day One of the interview, the second day was pretty quiet. I was told to wait in front of a meeting room. Around 30 minutes later, I entered the interview room and there were two interviewers sitting inside. One of them asked me why I wanted to leave AirAsia, especially since I had achieved the rank of senior cabin crew with the company. I replied, "I would like to explore different types of flight operations. I look forward to learning and would accept changes positively." The interview was great and I am grateful that I passed and managed to proceed to the final round—the uniform fitting. That was my very first time wearing the blue uniform and I felt excited yet a little anxious. After a round of catwalk and skin checks, we were given a short briefing in a meeting room where I received instructions on the documents I needed to prepare before signing the contract with Singapore Airlines.

One week later, I received a call from Singapore Airlines, and I had to undergo a medical examination in Kuala Lumpur. The medical examination was more or less the same as what AirAsia required; blood and urine tests were mandatory. There was also a vision test and physical inspection by the medical personnel on my limbs and abdomen, followed by an X-ray.

Around 3 weeks after the medical assessment, I was informed by Singapore Airlines via email that I had passed the medical examination and was to report to the SQ office in Kuala Lumpur on a given date. On the reporting date, my mum and sister accompanied me. There, I met a few other Malaysian candidates who also successfully passed their interview in Penang and they were my batch girls during training. We were briefed in detail with regards to the employment letter and the contract; it was a 5-year contract with a 2-year bond. We submitted our relevant documents[129] to the person-in-charge so that they could proceed with the application for our employment pass in Singapore.

Soaring the Sky

I felt heavy leaving my home and Malaysia. I am rather attached to my family. The feelings were different when I was a cabin crew with AirAsia and AirAsia X, because regardless of where I flew to, I would still go home after a flight duty. This time, I was going to be really away from home and my loved ones!

Singapore Airlines gave me a flight ticket with check-in luggage for a flight one week before our first day of training in Singapore. That was my first time flying with a premium airline. Furthermore, I met a few other candidates who were going to report for duty on the same day as I was. I felt excited and couldn't wait for this new phase of my life, and yet, my eyes were tearing because I had to say goodbye to my family. I boarded the plane with a heavy heart.

The cabin crew of the flight welcomed us warmly and they assisted us to our assigned seats. I couldn't tear my eyes from them—they looked so graceful with their blue *kebayas* and pleasant smiles. I couldn't believe that I would soon be one of them.

Upon arrival, we took a cab to the hotel provided by Singapore Airlines where we would be housed for the next 7 days, giving us ample time to search out accommodation in Singapore. The management had given us a date to attend a briefing at STC. On that day, we were briefed on what was required of us during training and throughout our employment. Following that, we received our employment passes.

After settling down in Singapore, I was about to begin my 14 weeks of training with Singapore Airlines. Singapore Airlines is an iconic symbol of Asian Hospitality, and their services have won multiple international awards. Their training is also well known as the most "intense" cabin crew training in the world. Subject to change, their training programme include[130]:

- Product Knowledge including Food & Beverage

- Service Procedures
- Passenger Handling
- Deportment & Grooming
- Language & Communication Skills
- Safety Equipment Procedures
- First Aid

Besides that, there were a lot of projects and presentations that required teamwork. And sometimes, we had to stay back after class to get our homework done. From these exercises, we learned to coordinate and support each other.

The cabin crew would start with 2 fleets: Airbus 330 and Boeing 777. Eventually, we were sent for additional fleet training on the Airbus 350, Airbus 380 and Boeing 787. Furthermore, SQ[131] cabin crew are also trained to serve in premium classes such as business class. To serve in the premium classes, cabin crew are required to undergo additional in-flight training that equips us to provide fine and personalised service. Although some people found it tough, I am grateful for the opportunity to learn and gain so much knowledge.

To maintain the esteemed standard of SQ service, we were not only trained to speak, walk and behave in a professional manner, but were also required to adhere to strict standards to maintain our image. Our grooming instructors would decide if we reached the bar, especially our make-up and hairstyles. Cabin crew are trained to comply strictly with the grooming guidelines such as the width of our hair bun, colour of the eyeshadow and many more. A "grooming card" was issued to each of us that detailed the approved colour of eye shadow, blusher, lipstick, nail polish and hairstyles. If we desired to change our "preset" image, we were required to get the approval from the grooming instructor first.

The In-flight Services Training in Singapore Airlines is detailed rather than intense. Cabin crew are not only well-trained in serving passengers, all the crew—from economy to premium class—are also trained on product knowledge. Moreover, we understood the different cooking methods such as simmering, boiling and stewing. This was so that we could explain the menu in detail to the passengers. Furthermore, we attended cultural talks with leaders from different nationalities to understand our passengers from different backgrounds. We were also required to provide community service during training, so that we were able to manage physically challenged people such as elderly passengers etc.

Just like any other airlines, we were also required to undergo safety and first aid training. A Singapore Airlines cabin crew may be rated on up to 5 fleets—the Airbus 330, Airbus 350, Airbus 380, Boeing 777 and Boeing 787. We had to sit and pass all the exams in order to operate each type of aircraft.

I learned so much during the 4 months of training and found it rather meaningful. Just like AirAsia, we had a graduation ceremony before flying as full-fledged crew for Singapore Airlines. We were required to work together as a team to plan and organise our own graduation ceremony at STC. All the instructors and a maximum of 2 family members per trainee were invited. I was grateful for not only my second graduation ever, but also for the award I received from Singapore Airlines—Best Groomed Award.

After training, we were required to fly under supervision[132] during normal line operations where our performance was monitored closely by our leaders during the 6 months of probation. We were evaluated on our safety knowledge, product knowledge, service skills, customer care, image and work relationship with colleagues.

On top of that, Singapore Airlines encourage their staff to learn, upskill and grow in the workplace by offering multiple training. For example, the Air Sommeliers[133]. Cabin crew are trained to recognise the different types of wines by colour and hue, brightness and clarity, taste, aromas and smells. Moreover, the airline also offered foreign language courses like French and German, not to mention barista and culinary training. The trainers that provided all these training were certified professionals and it was all free! All we had to do was to register for the courses on our day off.

The salary offered by Singapore Airlines was quite decent. We earned a basic salary of around 800 SGD to 1300 SGD (590 USD to 960 USD), not including flying allowance. For Malaysians, we were not paid accommodation allowance. Therefore, we had to find our own accomodation and rental in Singapore varied subject to location. Areas like Tampines, Pasir Ris and Simei are nearer to Changi Airport and are thus slightly more expensive. Meanwhile, places slightly further away from the airport were cheaper. Alternatively, one could share a unit with a landlord or other strangers. Another option was to pay a little extra in rent to enjoy the comfort and facilities of a condominium, or to rent an entire unit of flat to be shared amongst friends or batchmates. There are many options and should you find yourself in Singapore, choose the one that best meets your needs and budget.

I learned so much over my four and a half years with Singapore Airlines, and I will always be thankful for the experience. I am proud to have once been part of the acclaimed World's Best Cabin Crew[134]. However, the time came when I decided to go home to AirAsia, the place where I launched my flying career; the place that taught me to care and love people; the place I regarded as family.

Nothing was better than going home to family.

A few months later, I was grateful for the opportunity to join CAE[135] as a trainer. CAE Kuala Lumpur was founded in 2011 as the result of a joint venture between AirAsia and CAE[136]. CAE is now the operator of the training centre which offers initial and recurrent training to airline pilots on Airbus and Boeing platforms, as well as cabin crew training. In addition to its anchor customer AirAsia, CAE provides training to over 30 airlines from across the region[137].

Present day, I am mostly involved in training AirAsia crew and this has helped me grow closer to the crew and AirAsia. I aspire to keep learning so that I can serve CAE and AirAsia to the best of my abilities.

My Aviation Experience

The Reality of a Cabin Crew's Life

Here are some little secrets regarding what goes on behind the scenes...

Cabin crew are portrayed to have glamorous lifestyles, travelling and shopping around the world, staying at 5-star hotels, dining at luxurious restaurants and partying all the time. However, the fact is that as cabin crew, heavy responsibilities rest on our shoulders. Although your comfort during flight is very important to us, safety is our utmost priority.

In order to achieve a safe and pleasant flight, our preflight preparation is very important. For example, we self-brief on the aircraft type—different aircraft may require different SOP and safety procedures. We also learn the weather and local security procedures of the destination, especially if we are night-stopping overseas.

On top of that, I would study a little to refresh my knowledge on safety and emergency procedures, first aid, and SOP for in-flight services, as well as check my company email for the latest updates. When I was a newbie with Singapore Airlines, we were required to send a courtesy email to every member of the operating crew—a short introduction and also to humbly request the guidance of our fellow crew throughout the flight. Last but not least, I would iron my uniform and pack my bag. For turn-around flights[138], we were required to pack an extra set of uniform, proper attire, as well as toiletries in case of an unscheduled night stop. For flights that require us to nightstop overseas, we would pack our luggage according to the weather and length of our stay. Personally, "dry stores[139]" were always a must in my luggage, especially on long stays! There were times when our flight arrived late at night or early in the morning and most of the shops were closed. Sometimes, it snowed heavily outside the hotel; other times, I just felt too exhausted to step out of the room. Besides, some hotels do not provide 24-hour room service. In situations like these, a cup of instant noodles solved all my problems.

Before the flight, I would paint my nails while watching Korean dramas. This routine was especially the case when I was flying with Singapore Airlines as every female cabin crew were required to apply nail polish. Before I set my alarm and indulged in my beauty sleep, I would crosscheck all my flying documents and ensure that I had all my stuff packed accordingly.

I still remember my early days in AirAsia. The red planes were operating from LCCT[140] Sepang. That airport that was constantly crowded with passengers of different nationalities. For me, LCCT was a place that was full of humanity, sweat and tears. I was staying in Rawang back then. Subject to traffic, the journey from my home to the airport took around 3 to 4 hours. If I had to sign on for duty at 4 a.m., I would have to wake up to get ready for the flight at 1:30 a.m. There were also several times when I missed the last bus from LCCT after flight duty, so I had to wait for the first bus that would depart from LCCT at 4 a.m. the next day, and it would be 6 a.m. by the time I reached home. Then, I would have another duty at 2 p.m. on the same day. I know it sounds crazy. Besides, to save as much as I could, I chose to stay at home. Life got better for me when my family decided to move out of Rawang. With that, I spent less time travelling and was able to have quality rest before my flight duties. When I was in Singapore, I rented a place that was 10 to 15 minutes away from Changi Airport. I engaged a transport service that shuttled me to and from the airport. As cabin crew of Singapore Airlines, we were not allowed to travel by public transport—such as train and bus—while in uniform.

Despite that rule, the company only provided transport for duties with late sign-ons and early arrivals.

Back to the pre-flight duties. All cabin crew are required to attend a pre-flight briefing before flight. The senior cabin crew/ in-flight manager would begin the briefing by checking the validity of the crew's flying licences and travel documents. Subsequently, we would discuss the latest updates from the management and their vision for the flight. Next, the senior cabin crew/ in-flight manager would test us on safety and emergency procedures (SEP) and first aid to ensure that we have a proper grasp of the knowledge. Incompetent cabin crew may be offloaded from the flight. In AirAsia, the pilots would also brief the cabin crew on the weather and other relevant information.

Our first duty upon arriving at the aircraft is to ensure that all the safety equipment is serviceable, in the correct location and of the correct quantity. Then, we are to perform a thorough security check on the cabin, lavatory and galley. Any defect, missing equipment or foreign object is to be reported right away. Some of these equipment are very important as it is illegal for the plane to take-off without them.

Before we put on our brightest smiles to give you our warmest welcome, we had to ensure that the cabin and lavatories are clean, and that the food and beverages are properly catered. In Singapore Airlines which is a full-service airline, we also had to ensure that the pillows, blankets, newspapers, magazines, amenities, headset, etc, were sufficient. For premium classes, we had to ensure that the different types of crockery and glasses, selections of bread, meals, beverages, amenities etc, were in place.

After ensuring that the aircraft is in order, we would do a quick grooming check before positioning ourselves in the cabin to welcome our guests. During the boarding process, we are often asked to carry the passenger's cabin bag to stow in the overhead compartment. Now, cabin crew are more than happy to assist you, but we appreciate it if you give us a helping hand by sharing the weight of your bag with us instead of just leaving the bag entirely to the cabin crew. You are always welcomed to approach the cabin crew for help and we would always do our best to assist you.

However, we are grateful if you understand that helping you stow your luggage in the overhead compartment is not part of our duties.

Moving on, cabin crew are trained to be observant and alert to our surroundings. Other than assisting the guests to their seats, we are also trained to look out for passengers who might require special assistance such as guests travelling with an infant, guests in a wheelchair, elderly passengers, and passengers who might be drunk or sick before take-off. Crew are also to maintain a high level of situational awareness as sometimes, the aircraft is refuelled with passengers onboard, so there are some safety protocols to follow in such a situation. Moreover, the crew are also trained to address guests by their name and remember any special requests and preferences, especially when working in premium classes.

Most accidents happen during take-off and landing. Therefore, it is crucial that safety checks are carried out in the cabin to ensure that the passengers have their seatbelts securely fastened with their seats in an upright position, tray tables stowed and foot rest secured, armrests are down, window shades are drawn up, all belongings are stowed and portable electronic devices are switched off or in flight mode. Your safety is our utmost concern.

Here are a few common questions I get regularly:

Question 1: *Why must the seat be in an upright position? And why must the tray table, armrest and footrest be secured during take-off and landing?*

Answer: In case of an emergency, this will expedite the evacuation process as navigating around a reclined seat or opened tray table during or after a plane crash would be time-consuming.

Question 2: *Why must the window blinds be opened during take-off and landing?*

Answer: This is so that your eyes could adjust to the dark or the light outside, and you'll be able to react more quickly in case an evacuation is required. This is also the reason why the cabin lights are dimmed for take-off and landing. Besides that, the cabin crew want the outside condition to always be visible during take-off and landing. If any problem occurs with the engines or wings, we want to know which side is safe for evacuation. However, for your comfort, you may lower your shades after take-off.

Question 3: *Why must we store our bags in the overhead compartment?*

Answer: Stray bags may injure you or other passengers during turbulence, or they may slow down the evacuation process. Similarly, you are not allowed to keep your bag on your lap as it may hinder your ability to properly brace in case of an emergency.

Question 4: *Why must portable electronic devices be turned off or put on flight mode?*

Answer: Portable electronic devices may interfere with sensitive electronic components in the cockpit of the plane.

Given the technologies that we have nowadays, although most mobile phones do not emit strong radio waves, devices like laptops and even handheld gaming consoles may do so. As a result, usage of portable electronic devices during take-off and landing is banned in some regions because some airlines adhere to and enforce this safety protocol.

In-Flight Service

On top of safety, in-flight services are also very important in the airline industry. In-flight services refers to all services, free and paid, that aim to enhance the passengers' flying experience. It includes meals, snacks, beverages, duty-free shopping etc. We endeavour to always put customers first by not just meeting but also exceeding their needs, delighting them with quality services. To competently carry out a service, some planning is necessary. For example, we have to consider the layout of the cabin and seating arrangements. We also have to time the service of food and beverages, and the distribution of in-flight entertainment[141]. Good and professional service translates into happier customers; they feel warm, as if they are at home. This is how we attract loyal customers. In-flight services begin when the passengers first step into the aircraft, and last throughout the cruise, lull period, and ends only when the passengers disembark.

AirAsia has their own brand—*SANTAN* menu, a buy-on-board (BOB) initiative offering food and drinks for on board purchases. All you have to do is pre-book your meals through the website at least 24 hours before your scheduled flight departure time. In order to provide the passengers with a delicious culinary experience in the sky, the crew are trained to prepare the meals spot on at the correct temperature. Finally yet importantly, we create a fun and friendly shopping experience for the passengers.

Singapore Airlines operates an all wide-body passenger aircraft fleet—A330, A350, A380, B777 and B787. On top of the growing fleet of aircraft, Singapore Airlines is also well known for their onboard service. They offer 5 classes of service: suites, first class, business class, premium-economy class, and economy class. Singapore Airlines crew excel at providing a pleasant and luxurious flying experience across cabin classes, partly by offering a wide range of amenities, especially for children and infants. Pillows, blankets and toiletries are provided on long-haul flights. Besides, there is a wide selection of meals and beverages, not to forget Singapore Airlines' signature drink, the *Singapore Sling*. Furthermore, the flight is equipped with the latest in-flight entertainment—to be enjoyed on a widescreen LCD TV—in the form of movies, music, games and interactive programmes. Among SQ's best is the fine dining experience for passengers in the premium classes. Regional cuisines and wines are served on their respective routes. For example, a Japanese sector might serve *Hanakoireki* or *Kyo-kaiseki* cooking. Last but not least, Singapore Airlines tailor their services for a personalised experience. Passengers are addressed by name; the crew hang huge coats or jackets for passengers in a designated closet; the crew would take the children's meal orders and look out for elderly passengers; these are all in a day's work.

As cabin crew, it is essential that we know our menu inside out. Product knowledge is equally important. For example, we must be able to tell the passengers the wine's vintage. Our duty doesn't end after serving the meals. During lull periods, especially on long haul flights, we also frequently check the cabin for the passenger's welfare. The cabin crew are split into 2 teams on long-haul flights. While one team works, the other would rest in the crew bunks.

Some airlines practice post-flight briefing where the crew reflect and receive relevant feedback on the flight. If the crew night-stops at the destination, transport would be provided to and from the hotel. The room should be ready upon arrival at the hotel. However, there are times when the room is not ready and the crew would have to wait at the hotel lobby, completely exhausted. Apart from duty periods, we bond with the senior crew over lunch or dinner when on night-stops, especially during long stays.

More on My Personal Story…

I started flying when I was 18 years old. Have I ever regretted it? No. Never. Well, very often in life, there is no right or wrong; we do our best and be grateful for what we get.

Honestly though, when I remember what, or who, has been taken from me, I get depressed. I used to think that life would be much easier if daddy were still around. However, I can't change what has happened and the only way is forward. Having said that, I appreciate everything I have now.

AirAsia helped me grow into a person that is caring, loving, strong and humble. I was once a "high-flyer crew" in the company. I would rather go for flight and earn money than stay at home. Although the flying roster was tiring, I fully understood the business model of a low-cost airline.

In order to minimise the operating cost and allow maximum utilisation of the aircraft, AirAsia would turnaround[142] in a shorter than usual amount of time. If you have been to LCCT before, you would know what it was like. LCCT had minimum facilities and had the feel of a bus station—looked like a bus station too! You might have had times when you were unsure of which aircraft to board, or which way to the immigration. Or maybe you missed the bay number when the ground staff made the boarding announcement. Or, you might have boarded the wrong plane as 3 red AirAsia planes were parked along the same walkway, all departing to the same destination but with different flight numbers. Then, you probably saw a cabin crew standing at the walkway to direct the passengers to the immigration or arrival hall. You probably also saw another crew at the walkway, checking each passenger's boarding pass to avoid the passengers from boarding the wrong airplane.

Cabin crew are trained to multitask. On top of ensuring that passengers board the correct flight, the crew also observes if the passengers comply with tarmac rules, such as not using portable electronic devices while the aircraft is in the process of refuelling. At LCCT, air stairs were the only means to boarding and deplaning, so we had to ensure that umbrellas were handy for a rainy day. Regardless of the weather, may it be a sunny day when we had sweat dripping off our foreheads, or a rainy day when our uniform and shoes were soaked with water, we would still smile the moment passengers stepped into our cabin.

Unlike premium airlines, meals and beverages are not included in the fare at AirAsia. However, passengers may pre-book their meals before flight or purchase them on board. Besides, the passengers do not get souvenirs or toiletries. There is no complimentary cake or voucher for passengers on their honeymoon, or who are celebrating their birthday or anniversary. Despite that, we had creative ways of delighting our passengers by making handmade anniversary cards or singing the birthday song over the PA. Sometimes, we would even surprise our birthday passengers with little muffins that were paid for from our own pocket!

Do we party all the time? Partying is part and parcel of life when you are young; some crew party all day and night. Personally, I would prefer my beauty sleep to staying awake the whole night. Although the life of a crew may seem happening, flying crew are not allowed to consume alcohol 8 hours before a flight duty, as governed by the aviation regulations. Some airlines like Singapore Airlines and AirAsia even raised the bar to 10 hours.

Despite all the sweat and tears in the airline, there were also many sweet moments in between. For one, I am glad to have met someone who loved and cared for me when I needed him most. Nevertheless, I was young at that time and there were too many uncertainties. Therefore, I decided to leave in search for more experiences.

Singapore Airlines taught me so much in terms of knowledge and life experience. From safety, product knowledge to the finest of services. Regardless the type of fleet or if it was economy or business class, we aimed to touch our passengers' hearts with our service. On top of that, I am also grateful for my kind and loving housemates who were always there for me in Singapore.

During my first 2 years with Singapore Airlines, I was constantly looking forward to the middle of every month when the roster was published. Other than planning the dates that I could go back home to Malaysia, I would also plan for sightseeing at my favourite destinations. It was an extra bonus if I had a batchmate or friend rostered for the same flight. Few things beat seeing familiar names next to mine on the crew list. Nevertheless, before I got to visit and explore a destination, I had to first complete my duties on board and some of the flights were as long as 17 hours, not including the time I spent prepping and traveling. As each cabin crew has an important role on board, teamwork and taking ownership are the keys to a successful flight. We work hard while in uniform, and play hard when we're out of uniform.

Flying in the blue SQ uniform was like a dream. Singapore Airlines gave me the chance to see how big the world is; I visited places that I never dared to dream of ever seeing. Among my favourite places are:

New York, USA – The acclaimed city of the United States. There are many well-known districts and landmarks in this city such as Times Square, one of the world's busiest pedestrian zones; it is also home to the Broadway Theater District and a major hub of the world's entertainment industry. Then there's Grand Central Terminal, located on 42nd Street and Park Avenue in Midtown Manhattan—a must go for its insta-worthy aesthetics. Of course, the cupcakes in Magnolia Bakery at Grand Central Terminal are equally esteemed! Our hotel was walking distance to Times Square and *Shake Shack*, an American casual restaurant that serves delicious burgers. If you are a beef lover, you may want to try their *Shack Burger*. And if a good breakfast or brunch is what you seek, *Sarabeth's Restaurant* is highly recommended; they serve delicious eggs benedicts.

Los Angeles, USA - Other than New York, I was lucky to have made memories by operating a flight with my batch girl to Los Angeles. We rented a sports car—a Mustang—and drove around Hollywood, the mecca of the entertainment industry, not to mention tourist-magnet. We also drove to Santa Monica and had our dinner there, against a beautiful sunset. That was my best Los Angeles night-stop experience ever!

Zurich, Switzerland – The largest city in Switzerland. I personally recommend Zurich Lake, Lucerne and Mt.

Titlis. Alternatively, you can spend your afternoon at a café named *Confiserie Sprüngli* to enjoy their coffee and sweet treats. On top of that, *Blausee Schweiz*, a small lake in Switzerland, is well-known for being scenic with its deep-blue crystal-clear water—pretty as a picture! If you ever do visit Switzerland, consider a road trip to slowly drink in the scenery.

Munich, Germany - The capital of Germany and the most populous city of Bavaria[143]. Places like *Neuschwanstein* Castle, Prague and Salzburg should not be missed. And if you are there during Christmas time, there is a variety of food and drinks at the Christmas Market that you must try! I love the *Gebrannte Mandeln* (roasted almond), *Stollen* (fruit and nut loaf), *Paradiesapfel* (candied apple) and *Gluhwein* (a traditional drink for winter. It is an alcoholic beverage that is served hot or warm, also known as spice wine). Even the baked potatoes with extra cheese and ham became extra delicious during the cold winter! Last but not least, the beer and sausages in Germany are unforgettable.

Disneyland - One of my childhood dreams was to visit Disneyland. I am grateful that Singapore Airlines gave me the opportunity to visit not one but three Disneylands. During one of my trips to Disneyland Paris, it was snowing heavily and the weather was freezing cold. Yet, two other crew and I decided to spend our trip at Disneyland rather than shopping in Paris. Yes, we looked like close friends on a trip but in fact, we just met 12 hours prior! That is another strength that cabin crew possess: we make friends after just one flight. At Disneyland, the outdoor facilities were mostly closed due to the heavy snow. We were a little disappointed as we could only enjoy the indoor rides. Nevertheless, we were so excited when the fireworks show began against the tune of "Let It Go" from the popular Disney Film, *Frozen*. The snow and the song actually made the fireworks blaze even brighter in the night sky and I would always remember that magical moment for the rest of my life.

I've visited so many places. I've spent Christmas shopping in London. I've enjoyed the sun and beach at the paradise in the Indian Ocean: Maldives. I've also visited the former capital of the Indian state of Gujarat: Ahmedabad. What's beautiful about this city is not just the art and culture, but the people; they are friendly and helpful. Similarly, I've been to Dubai, a city in the United Arab Emirates that is known for luxury shopping, ultramodern architecture and a lively nightlife. I've visited Beijing, Seoul, Nagoya, London, Amsterdam, Rome… Want to follow my adventures? Follow me on Instagram *@ceci.magic*!

The Other Side of Flying

Cabin crew are often switching through time zones. For example the time zone in Singapore is GMT +8, whereas Moscow is GMT +3 and it's GMT -5 in Houston. Although we enjoy exploring new places, there were also times when we were just too tired to go anywhere and we called this "hibernation". I would normally stock up on my "dry stores" and retreat to my room to binge on a drama series or read a book. I was content with simply enjoying some quiet me-time, maybe a cup of hot coffee near London Bridge with my favourite book and camera.

Sometimes, I would be away for a week or even longer. During times like that, I felt homesick and missed all the food and people in Malaysia. There is nowhere like home! Malaysia is a melting pot of different races, cultures and food. The multicultural setting that I grew up in has taught me to respect others, be understanding and to be able to cope with changes. In the same vein, as a Malaysian, I am spoiled for choice when it comes to food. I can enjoy *Nasi Lemak* for breakfast, Chicken Rice for lunch, *Kuih Nyonya* during tea time, *Biryani* Rice for dinner and *Teh Tarik* for supper. In some other countries, the shops and restaurants close by 6 p.m. But in Malaysia, *Mamak*[144] stalls stay open around the clock. I am ardently proud to be Malaysian!

Nonetheless, cabin crew are not perfect, and we do screw up from time to time. There were several times when I forgot a passenger's request and only remembered after lying down on my bed. At that moment, I felt like my heart stopped for a second. There were also moments when I felt like a superhero! On top of serving coffee and tea, I juggled a myriad of tasks: checking on the welfare of my passengers as I walked down the aisle, tending to the cleanliness of the cabin and lavatory, collecting trash, being alert of my surroundings so that I could react quickly in case of an accident or emergency. I have also experienced awkward moments on board. There was a couple on honeymoon who started fighting as soon as the plane took off, and they refused to sit next to each other throughout the flight. All things considered, nothing beat the moment a passenger brightened my day with a compliment, telling me how much they appreciated my hard work.

Behind the scenes of a seemingly luxurious life of flying is the pain of lost time with family and loved ones. I am missing from countless wedding dinner and birthday party pictures. Very often, cabin crew miss out on *Hari Raya*, Chinese New Year, Christmas etc, festivals. For me, the toughest part wasn't being absent during festive seasons, but failing to be there for a sick family member when they needed me the most.

On top of zapping around from time zone to time zone and missing a lot of anecdotes, cabin crew are sometimes also required to be on standby and it is considered a duty. Subject to airline operations, some standby duties are shorter shifts, some are for 24-hour stretches, and some require the crew to be at the office. 24-hour standbys were always my least preferred. Although the standby was at home and it might seem like I was able to rest, the possibility of getting activated for flight was constantly looming above my head and it could get quite stressful. There were times when we got activated at the last minute to replace another cabin crew. There was once when I received a call from the office during my 24-hour standby duty at 11:55 p.m., activating me for a departure to Zurich at 1:30 a.m. I had to shower, pack, dress, and rush to the airport. At the airport, I would have to clear immigration and make my way to the aircraft parking bay, and I had to do all that within that short period of time. I hurried to get ready and missed packing certain items as I wasn't sure how the weather in Zurich was like, nor the length of my stay there. I was in such a rush that I only had time to apply make-up inside the cab.

I had spent almost 5 years in Singapore when I decided to return to Malaysia. Never in my life did I miss home so much before. I had seen the world and learned so much about life. I felt so blessed and thankful for everything that had happened. But it was time to go home, and so I did. I was glad to be back in red, flying with AirAsia once again. This time around, I was more matured at handling situations onboard. It was so much fun flying with people that I know or used to fly with. However, something lingered in me: I wanted to meet *him* again and wondered how he was doing in life.

After a few months back in AirAsia, I was given an opportunity to join CAE as an instructor. It was an opportunity to learn and grow, and to guide my juniors by sharing with them all that I had learned during my flying days. I accepted the offer. Since then, CAE has given me the opportunity to participate in many development programmes, such as *Train the Trainer Course* and *Dangerous Good Regulations Category 6*. I was also given the opportunity to experience a Search and Rescue exercise, an exercise that is pure action with a concoction of aircraft, maritime vessels, and disaster and medical machinery, all to test how effective and prepared the personnels from enforcement agencies are. Besides that, I also went through Jungle and Sea Survival Training with the Special Malaysia Disaster Assistance and Rescue Team (SMART). Working with the military personnel was a great experience for me. I learned so much, and not just about teamwork. I also learned to be compassionate and to build others up.

To the men and women in uniform, especially those I worked with, I say: Thank you for serving our country. We have a safe home because of you. You are our heroes.

Besides, I am grateful for all the talented instructors at CAE who have guided me till this point. They have made learning exciting and I aspire to be like them. I hope to keep sharing and building.

In this job, there is no alternative; be humble, be kind, be brave, and always love and care for your crew and passengers.

Some people may think that this is an unintelligent job, or that cabin crew are nothing more than waitresses in the sky. Allow me to debunk that myth. Most airlines require their cabin crew to have at least a diploma or sometimes even a degree. If the candidate does not meet that requirement, they require at least some relevant job experience. Cabin crew are trained to ensure the safety and comfort of passengers on board. They undergo a minimum of 3 months of training that include safety, first aid, in-flight services, etc. Moreover, there is a mandatory annual recurrent training that every cabin crew must go through to stay current.

As cabin crew, we meet people from all walks of life. There are moments of tears, tenderness, bitterness and sweetness. Through my years of flying, I have experienced engine failure and landing gear failure where the crew were instructed to prepare for emergency landing. I occupied myself with the tasks as I tried to stay calm. My tears started to fall the moment I returned to my crew seat; one minute, everything was smooth-sailing and then suddenly out of the blue, my whole world came crashing down. Then, there was a time when I was required to perform CPR on a passenger who was not breathing and had no pulse. Other times, I've had fainted passengers, and passengers that got injured due to clear air turbulence. Once, I had to perform crowd control as there was suspicious smoke rising from the waste bin in the lavatory. There was also a time when an old couple who could only speak Chinese urgently needed to use the lavatory just as the aircraft was approaching the runway. I tried to stop them, but they couldn't hear me above the engine sound. Therefore, I decided to release my seatbelt and assisted them to the nearest available seat. Subsequently, I managed to return to my seat right before the aircraft touched down. After the flight, I was given a long briefing as I jeopardised my own safety. I accepted it and considered it a learning opportunity. I wasn't thinking much at that point of time. All I had in mind was the safety of the old couple as they were not prepared for situations like that. Without the safety of their seat belts, they might get injured if the aircraft jerked violently. Thankfully, we landed uneventfully. One month later, I received a compliment letter from the daughter of the old couple. The long appreciation letter really touched my heart. On a separate occasion, a passenger under my care died onboard. The passenger showed no signs of life after the airplane landed. I was just serving him breakfast before landing and the next moment, he was not breathing. From that incident, I learned that life is unpredictable and we should always be grateful for what we have.

All the experiences that I had have built me into who I am today. I have learned to be grateful, kind, humble, sincere, brave and to love and care for the people around me. I endeavour to become a better person. I sincerely wish that one day, you may also spread your wings and paint your literal or metaphorical sky with your dream.

I always tell my trainees this: To be a star, you must be humble enough to learn. Be strong enough to accept challenges and never take "no" for an answer. Be kind. Help and love those around you. Be brave enough to live in the darkness, and do every one of these sincerely with your whole heart.

And I believe that full-heartedly.

I came across a quote once: *One day, someone will walk into your life and make it right.*

And on that note, I will keep an open heart. Until we meet again...

Part Three

Inside the Trading Room

Chapter 1.

<u>Why Invest?</u>

The Importance of Passive Income

Different people have different financial goals. Some want to retire early, some want a big mansion, others want a fancy fast car, while yet others want to achieve financial freedom. There are two ways to make money in this modern world. The first way involves working for another person or for yourself, where you exchange your labour and time for money. The second way is by putting your money to work, investing in financial assets that will grow in value over time, even while you are sleeping. The major drawback of the first way is that money stops coming in when you stop working or become unable to work. Furthermore, there are only 24 hours a day, so there is only that much work you can do in a day. To boot, your productivity often declines as you age, leading to less output. Productivity peaks when a person enters his or her 40s and declines rapidly after 60.

Months after joining AirAsia, I realised that piloting is a highly specialised job. This means that pilots are specialists rather than generalists. A specialist is a person who knows a lot about very little and is trained rigorously to perform a handful of tasks. On the other hand, a generalist, a person who knows a little about a lot, is trained to do multiple jobs.

In the aviation industry, some pilots have lost their jobs due to deterioration in health, failure of their biannual simulator proficiency check, or setbacks in the airline industry such as the effect of Covid-19 on the industry. Many of these are beyond the control of pilots. We all know some athletes who went broke after their sports career ended. Therefore, it is crucial that every specialist learns a different skill set or establishes a passive income in case the undesirable happens.

Freedom is a precious thing. And to achieve real freedom, you must first achieve financial freedom. If you have to work everyday for money, you don't have freedom. All things considered, investing is a great way to achieve financial freedom. Warren Buffett said, "If you don't find a way to make money while you sleep, you will work until you die."

Passive income comes in various forms. It can be a dividend received from a stock investment, rental income from a rental apartment, monthly distribution from a pension fund, or royalties from a patent, movie, song or book. It was reported that Jin Yong, a well-known Chinese martial arts novel author, often referred to by the media as "the richest man of letters in the last five thousand years", received over 40 million dollars a year in royalty payments for his novels[145].

In 2015, I successfully convinced my father to install solar panels on his factory's roof. Apart from making the earth greener and benefiting from favourable tax incentives[146], the factory has also gotten cooler because the solar panels reflect solar radiation. However, the most exciting part of this is that the solar system generates about RM 6,000 (USD 1,400) in passive income every month. This is a great example of a steady stream of passive income.

Stock

In Malaysia, when it comes to investing, the only asset that pops up in the minds of the general public is real estate. Buying an apartment and renting it out for monthly rental income is perceived by many as the best investment option there is. Stocks, on the other hand, are often regarded as risky and a lousy investment. For many generations, stocks have been thought of as gambling by the majority of the population. A distrust in stocks is the prevailing Malaysian attitude that has been passed on from generation to generation. If the idea of investing in the stock market terrifies you, you are not alone. This perception is primarily attributed to a lack of knowledge and experience. Similarly, to a person living in a remote village, flying is viewed as a risky and dangerous means of transportation.

When we were little, our parents probably told us that stock-investing is risky and should be avoided. Nonetheless, we should seek wisdom from those who have studied the subject and thrived at it. You should consult a tax adviser about taxation and not a pilot. Likewise, we should seek the advice of financial experts and bankers instead of our parents who often have little or no investing experience. Moreover, do you know that financial institutions such as insurance companies, endowment funds, and pension funds like the Employee Provident Fund (EPF) of Malaysia also invest in stocks? So, it is mindless to regard stock-investing as risky if even these institutions consider it safe.

A stock, or a share of stock, is a financial security that represents the ownership of a fraction of a company. A shareholder is entitled to a portion of the company's assets and earnings. Shareholders also have voting rights when electing the board of directors. They have the final say on company policies too.

The stocks of public companies[147] are traded predominantly on stock exchanges. For example, Maybank stocks are traded on the Bursa stock exchange and Amazon stocks are traded on the Nasdaq stock exchange. Stock exchanges are governed and heavily regulated by the Security Commission (SC) or in the case of the US, the Security Exchange Commission (SEC), to prevent fraud and protect investors.

Corporations issue stocks, usually through an underwriter like a financial institution or an investment bank, via an initial public offering (IPO) to raise funds for business expansion and/or debt payment. An IPO refers to the process of offering the shares of a private company to the public for the first time. It allows a private company to raise funds from the public. Most new startups prefer IPO to bank loans for the simple reason that they would be obligated to pay their loan and failure to do so could lead to the seizure of the company's assets, not to mention the risk of bankruptcy.

When you buy a share of stock, you are actually buying a tiny fraction of the company's assets and future earnings[148]. For example, if a company has 100 shares of stock outstanding and you own 10 shares, you are entitled to 10% of the company's assets and earnings.

Historically, stocks have outperformed all other financial assets in the long run. Historical data shows that since 1926, the general stock market has yielded a 10 to 11% average annual return after inflation[149]. A share price rises when there are more buyers than sellers, and falls when there are more sellers than buyers. However, in the long run, it is the company's earnings that drive stock prices. If the management of a public company thinks their stock is undervalued, they might engage a share buyback programme to reward their shareholders. Warren Buffett, a legendary investor, business tycoon and philanthropist, is an advocate of the buy and hold strategy. Since it is extremely hard to time the market, something even the world's best hedge fund managers and speculators fail to do, he believes that the average investor can outperform most fund managers in the long run by investing in a low-cost exchange traded fund (ETF) that tracks the major stock market indices[150]. An ETF is an investment fund that is traded on a stock exchange that holds a wide range of stocks, bonds or commodities. A stock ETF that tracks the underlying stock index, such as the SPDR S&P 500 ETF (SPY), owns a basket of securities in the stock index. For example, the holdings of SPY comprise all the 500 stocks in the S&P 500 index. Buying SPY is equivalent to investing in all the 500 companies stocks, albeit at a much lower cost.

Dollar-Cost Averaging Strategy

Miss Lucile Tomlinson, the author of one of the best-selling personal investing books of all time, *Successful Investing Formulas*, said, "No one has yet to discovered any other formula for investing which can be used with so much confidence of ultimate success, regardless of what may happen to security prices, as dollar cost averaging."[151]

On average, a person works for 45 years. Assume that a person consistently invests 1,000 dollars a year into the S&P 500 every year for 45 years. Say he started at the age of 20 in 1975. This is what his current portfolio would look like (for simplicity sake, transaction costs and brokerage fees are not included):

Age	Year	S&P 500 Performance	Portfolio
20	1975	31.55%	1,316 USD
21	1976	19.15%	2,759 USD
22	1977	-11.50%	3,327 USD
23	1978	1.06%	4,373 USD
24	1979	12.31%	6,034 USD
25	1980	25.77%	8,847 USD
26	1981	-9.73%	8,888 USD
27	1982	14.76%	11,348 USD

28	1983	17.27%	14,480 USD
29	1984	1.40%	15,697 USD
30	1985	26.33%	21,094 USD
31	1986	14.62%	25,324 USD
32	1987	2.03%	26,858 USD
33	1988	12.40%	31,312 USD
34	1989	27.25%	41,118 USD
35	1990	-6.56%	39,355 USD
36	1991	26.31%	50,972 USD
37	1992	4.46%	54,290 USD
38	1993	7.06%	59,193 USD
39	1994	-1.54%	59,266 USD
40	1995	34.11%	80,823 USD
41	1996	20.26%	98,401 USD
42	1997	31.01%	130,225 USD
43	1998	26.67%	166,223 USD
44	1999	19.53%	199,881 USD
45	2000	-10.14%	180,512 USD
46	2001	-13.04%	157,843 USD
47	2002	-23.37%	121,721 USD
48	2003	26.38%	155,095 USD
49	2004	8.99%	170,128 USD

50	2005	3.00%	176,262 USD
51	2006	13.62%	201,405 USD
52	2007	3.53%	209,550 USD
53	2008	-38.49%	129,509 USD
54	2009	23.45%	161,113 USD
55	2010	12.78%	182,832 USD
56	2011	0.00%	183,832 USD
57	2012	13.41%	209,617 USD
58	2013	29.60%	272,960 USD
59	2014	11.39%	305,164 USD
60	2015	-0.73%	303,929 USD
61	2016	9.54%	334,019 USD
62	2017	19.42%	400,080 USD
63	2018	-6.24%	376,053 USD
64	2019	28.88%	485,945 USD

Source: Wikipedia – S&P 500 Index. I have checked that the maths is correct.

His total investment capital was only 45,000 USD (1,000 USD x 45 years) and yet his investment return over the 45-year period was 440,945 USD (485,945 USD – 45,000 USD).

The performance shown above doesn't even include the reinvestment of dividends. A dividend is the distribution of a company's earnings or excess cash to its shareholders in the form of cash or additional stocks. The reinvestment of dividends would have produced a much better result, as shown below:

Age	Year	S&P 500 Performance	Your Portfolio
20	1975	37.20%	1,372 USD
21	1976	23.84%	2,938 USD
22	1977	-7.18%	3,655 USD
23	1978	6.56%	4,960 USD
24	1979	18.44%	7,059 USD
25	1980	32.50%	10,678 USD
26	1981	-4.92%	11,104 USD
27	1982	21.55%	14,712 USD
28	1983	22.56%	19,257 USD
29	1984	6.27%	21,527 USD
30	1985	31.73%	29,675 USD
31	1986	18.67%	36,402 USD
32	1987	5.25%	39,365 USD
33	1988	16.61%	47,070 USD
34	1989	31.69%	63,303 USD
35	1990	-3.10%	62,310 USD

36	1991	30.47%	82,601 USD
37	1992	7.62%	89,971 USD
38	1993	10.08%	100,141 USD
39	1994	1.32%	102,476 USD
40	1995	37.58%	142,362 USD
41	1996	22.96%	176,278 USD
42	1997	33.36%	236,418 USD
43	1998	28.58%	305,272 USD
44	1999	21.04%	370,712 USD
45	2000	-9.10%	337,886 USD
46	2001	-11.89%	298,592 USD
47	2002	-22.10%	233,382 USD
48	2003	28.68%	301,603 USD
49	2004	10.88%	335,527 USD
50	2005	4.91%	353,050 USD
51	2006	15.79%	409,955 USD
52	2007	5.49%	433,516 USD
53	2008	-37.00%	273,745 USD
54	2009	26.46%	347,443 USD
55	2010	15.06%	400,918 USD
56	2011	2.11%	410,399 USD
57	2012	16.00%	477,222 USD

58	2013	32.39%	633,118 USD
59	2014	13.69%	720,929 USD
60	2015	1.38%	731,892 USD
61	2016	11.96%	820,546 USD
62	2017	21.83%	1,000,889 USD
63	2018	-4.38%	958,006 USD
64	2019	31.49%	1,260,997 USD

Source: Wikipedia – S&P 500 Index. I have checked that the maths is correct.

The difference that results from simply reinvesting the dividends over the 45-year period in the same stock market is staggering: an extra gain of 775,052 USD (1,260,997 USD – 485,945 USD).

Let's apply the same dollar cost averaging strategy on Hang Seng Index (excluding the reinvestment of dividends), a market value-weighted stock index that comprises a selection of the largest companies in Hong Kong, to see if it works.

Age	Year	Hang Seng Performance	Your Portfolio
20	1975	104.55%	2,046 USD
21	1976	27.91%	3,896 USD
22	1977	-9.75%	4,418 USD

23	1978	22.64%	6,645 USD
24	1979	77.47%	13,567 USD
25	1980	67.57%	24,411 USD
26	1981	-4.60%	24,242 USD
27	1982	-44.24%	14,075 USD
28	1983	11.63%	16,828 USD
29	1984	89.62%	33,805 USD
30	1985	45.99%	50,812 USD
31	1986	46.55%	75,931 USD
32	1987	-10.34%	68,976 USD
33	1988	16.70%	81,662 USD
34	1989	5.55%	87,250 USD
35	1990	6.63%	94,101 USD
36	1991	42.08%	135,119 USD
37	1992	28.28%	174,614 USD
38	1993	115.67%	378,746 USD
39	1994	-31.10%	261,645 USD
40	1995	22.98%	323,001 USD
41	1996	33.53%	432,638 USD
42	1997	-20.29%	345,653 USD
43	1998	-6.29%	324,848 USD
44	1999	68.80%	550,032 USD

45	2000	-11.00%	490,418 USD
46	2001	-24.50%	371,021 USD
47	2002	-18.21%	304,276 USD
48	2003	34.92%	411,878 USD
49	2004	13.15%	467,172 USD
50	2005	4.54%	489,427 USD
51	2006	34.20%	658,153 USD
52	2007	39.31%	918,266 USD
53	2008	-48.27%	475,536 USD
54	2009	52.02%	724,430 USD
55	2010	5.32%	764,023 USD
56	2011	-19.97%	612,248 USD
57	2012	22.91%	753,743 USD
58	2013	2.87%	776,404 USD
59	2014	1.28%	787,355 USD
60	2015	-7.16%	731,909 USD
61	2016	0.39%	735,767 USD
62	2017	35.99%	1,001,929 USD
63	2018	-13.61%	866,431 USD
64	2019	9.07%	946,107 USD

Source: Wikipedia – Hang Seng Index. I have checked that the maths is correct.

The total investment capital was the same 45,000 USD (1,000 USD x 45 years). However, the absolute investment return was 901,107 USD (946,107 USD – 45,000 USD).

Note: Past performance is not an indicator of future returns.

Despite several economic downturns during the 45-year period like the Black Monday of 1987, the Asian financial crisis of 1997, the 9/11 terrorist attacks of 2001, the dot-com crash of the early 2000s, the Great Recession of 2008, Brexit, the European sovereign debt crisis, the SARS outbreak, trade war tension between the U.S. and China, and countless natural disasters such as tsunamis and major earthquakes, both portfolios managed to produce sizeable returns. The above example doesn't even take into account the reinvestment of stock dividends. If included, the returns would be much higher. This strategy has not only stood the test of time, but has proven to be the best long-term investing approach. If followed with discipline, it eliminates the one thing that causes most investment losses: emotions. If the investment was made monthly or weekly instead of annually as per the above example, the dollar cost averaging strategy would be more advantageous and yield better results.

That is the power of compounding. The world's arguably greatest scientist, Sir Albert Einstein, was reported to have described compounding interest as the "eighth wonder of the world"[152]. Compounding means the process of reinvesting dividends or capital gains at the same rate of return as the principal investment over time, which multiplies an investor's return at an ever-accelerating rate. It is a great technique in making your money work hard for you. Every investor should use this technique to their advantage through a disciplined investment strategy.

Since most people don't have the expertise to pick winning stocks nor time to read financial reports[153], I recommend the dollar-cost averaging or passive investing strategy for any long term investor, in which the investor puts a fixed amount of money into an investment at regular intervals, for example, every week or every month, regardless of the ups and downs of the market. This strategy aims to reduce the impact of volatility by spreading out the investment over a long time period. When stocks are expensive, the investor buys less units of shares. When stocks are cheap, with the same amount of money, he buys more shares. This strategy also keeps the investor from buying too much at market peaks and too little at market bottoms, hence ensuring that the average purchase price remains low.

Another advantage of the dollar-cost averaging strategy is that it refrains investors from frequent or excessive trading, which incurs higher brokerage fees and transaction cost that could eat into the profits.

Short term stock prices are driven by the news, investors' sentiments and emotions, notably greed and fear. However, in the long term, they are driven by fundamentals. As long as the economy is growing healthily at a steady pace, the future prospects of the country are promising, and the demographics are favourable, the stock market is expected to continue its upward trend in the long run. It is no wonder that some insurance companies, sovereign wealth funds, endowment funds and pension funds adopt this strategy when investing in stocks.

Paul Samuelson, the first American economist to win the Nobel Memorial Prize in Economic Sciences, said, "Investing should be more like watching paint dry or watching grass grow. If you want excitement, take 800 dollars and go to Las Vegas."[154]

Bond

A bond is a form of debt. It is a fixed income instrument issued by a federal government, state government, government agency or corporation. When a person purchases a government bond, he or she lends money to the government and becomes a creditor. The government in turn promises the investor an interest. Upon the maturity date, the principal amount of the bond must be paid in full or risk default. Governments and government agencies typically issue bonds to raise funds for finance projects and operations, such as to build a bridge or local hospital. Corporations, likewise, issue bonds to raise funds for business expansion and operations. If a company goes under, after paying off its creditors by selling the remaining assets and inventory, what is left will be used to pay bondholders. Finally, shareholders will receive what is left, if there is any.

Government bonds are generally considered to be very safe, but they pay a lower interest rate than corporate bonds. If the government bonds are denominated in its own currency and the government has an independent central bank, the possibility of the government defaulting on its debts is close to zero. This explains why Greece, whose debts were denominated in Euro and has no independent central bank, declared bankruptcy in 2011. Governments with their own central banks and whose debts are denominated in their own currencies can always print money to service their debts, or issue new bonds to service old ones.

Corporate bonds, to compete with safer government bonds for investors' money, usually pay a higher interest rate. Since not all companies are created equal, and some carry less credit risk than others, the interest rate paid varies with the creditworthiness and financial condition of the company. Companies on the verge of bankruptcy or in poor financial health usually pay a much higher interest rate to attract investors because their bonds are practically junk to the investors.

To make bond investing simple, bond rating agencies[155] determine the safety and likelihood of default of an organisation and categorise them using letters, numbers or symbols[156]. A bond rated AAA is considered the safest and chances of default are negligible, whereas bonds with a CC rating are thought of as junk and carry significant default risk. In addition, short-term bonds carry less risk than long-term bonds, which explains why long-term bonds pay a higher interest rate.

Bonds are traded freely on the market, primarily the over-the-counter (OTC) market. Like stocks, their prices change on a daily basis under the same rule of supply and demand. Bond prices have an inverse relationship with interest rates. When interest rates increase, bond prices decrease and vice versa. As an example, when a central bank hikes the interest rate, existing government bonds that pay the old interest rate always fall in value, since investors would prefer to buy newly issued bonds with a higher interest rate. Conversely, when a central bank lowers the interest rate, existing government bonds always rise in value, since they offer a higher yield than the newly issued ones.

Given their safe and conservative nature, insurance companies and pension funds tend to invest a large portion of their capital in bonds. Bonds are also a suitable investment option for retirees who rely on a stream of steady income for their medical and living expenses. Nonetheless, bonds are less attractive in a low interest rate environment, like the one we are living in now. In order to keep up with their outlays, insurance companies and pension funds might shift a portion of their investment into bonds that pay a higher interest rate, which, of course, also means a higher risk of default. However, other than default risk, bond investors face another formidable enemy: inflation.

Inflation vs Deflation

"Americans are getting stronger. Twenty years ago, it took two people to carry ten dollar's worth of groceries. Today, a five-year-old can do it." – Henny Youngman[157].

Inflation means a sustained rise in the general price level of goods and services in an economy. As a result, a unit of money buys less and less over time. It is a reflection of the falling purchasing power of the currency that leads to rising prices, since goods and services are measured in currencies. Hence, it can be said that rising prices is the symptom while the falling currency value is the cause.

Inflation occurs when money supply outgrows the economy, leading to more money for the same amount of goods and services. Inflation also happens when the demand for money falls, or when spending by the public suddenly increases, leading to more demand for goods and services.

According to the U.S. Bureau of Labour Statistics, ever since the Federal Reserve, the central bank of the U.S., was created in 1913, the U.S. dollar has lost over 95% of its purchasing power[158]. The devaluation of the dollar was further exacerbated in 1971 when President Richard Nixon ended the Bretton Woods agreement[159] and the convertibility of the U.S. dollar into gold. Since then, all the paper money in the world is basically fiat currencies. Personally, this is by far the most significant event that has ever happened in the 20th century; it has played a critical role in every investment decision I've made. I believe the end of the Bretton Woods system has had and will continue to have far reaching consequences in the world we live in. Central banks around the world now have the ability to create money out of thin air at virtually no cost. That's why I recommend that my clients save their wealth in real money, namely precious metals like gold, silver and platinum; money that central banks can't print.

People who wish to save their wealth in precious metals can do so by buying precious metals ETFs that are backed by physical gold or silver, or opening a gold or silver savings account at the local bank. Alternatively, they can purchase physical gold or silver bullions from any precious metals bullion shop. Contrary to popular belief, precious metals are not an investment. They don't produce income the way a company or farmland does. Hence, they shouldn't be viewed as an investment vehicle to generate wealth. The primary purpose of saving your money in gold and silver is to preserve wealth, not create wealth.

In times of financial turmoil, central banks around the world would step on the monetary accelerator, first by lowering interest rates, then by creating money out of thin air to purchase massive quantities of securities[160] in order to prevent a liquidity crisis[161] and stabilise[162] the financial market. This kicking-the-can-down-the road approach simply delays the inevitable and could result in unintended consequences. Since every politician has a term of only 4 to 5 years, most would prefer to adopt this drinking-poison-to-cure-thirst strategy and let their successor deal with the mess. They fail to consider that if they print more money than the economy can take, it will erode the value of the currency and result in monetary inflation.

The gradual loss of purchasing power of money has a negative impact on the cost of living for the general public, especially those who live on a fixed income, such as a pensioner. As inflation erodes the value of their income and wealth, pensioners, bond holders, bank depositors, savers, lenders and those who live on a fixed income, in actual fact get poorer over time in terms of purchasing power. In contrast, inflation works in the favour of debtors, borrowers and commodities producers because inflation reduces the real value of their debts and raises the value of their assets which they can then sell at a higher price. On top of that, inflation promotes investment and business activities. Knowing that the general level of prices will go up and the purchasing power of cash will decline over time, consumers and businesses tend to make purchases now rather than on a later date. They engage in productive activities that will produce a return higher than the inflation rate.

The 1980s saw massive inflations in the U.S., caused primarily by an expansion in monetary base and a sharp rise in crude oil prices. Gold prices soared dramatically to hit 850 USD an ounce, or 2,246 USD in today's money, after adjusting for inflation. Persistent double-digit inflation threatened to topple the status of the U.S. dollar as the world's reserve currency, and that could've resulted in unprecedented consequences. President Richard Nixon adopted price and wage controls to counter inflation but failed miserably. To break the back of inflation, Federal Reserve Board chairman Paul Volcker took painful but necessary steps to rein in the runaway inflation by hiking fed funds rates to levels not seen since the universe began. This bold step eventually returned the inflation rate to normal and stable levels, restoring the credibility of the U.S. dollar. Since that event, inflation targeting has been the main agenda of monetary policies for countries around the world.

Deflation, however, is the complete opposite of inflation. Deflation is a sustained decline of the general price level of goods and services over time where a unit of money buys more and more of them. Deflation typically occurs when the money supply and credit in an economy falls in relative to the amount of goods and services it can buy. On the surface, deflation benefits consumers because they can buy more with less over time. However, for decades now, deflation has been viewed by most economists as a monster. In an economy where deflation prevails, in anticipation of lower prices in the future, consumers will defer spending in the hope of eventually buying at a lower price. As one's spending is someone else's income, this slows down economic activities and would, in turn, result in yet further decline in prices. The whole process is self-reinforcing and will ultimately result in high unemployment and subsequently cause other social problems. In addition, deflation increases the real value of debts and makes debt servicing more costly. As a result, global central banks usually have a mandate to promote an optimum level of inflation.

Apart from the contraction in money supply, three other factors have contributed to falling prices. Firstly, vast improvements in productivity and technological innovations and advancements over the years have greatly suppressed the cost of living. For example, a TV set today costs only a fraction of its price a decade ago. Computers, home appliances, electronic devices, and many others are a lot cheaper than they were years ago. Secondly, these facilities come with improved features and functions. Emails, WhatsApp, WeChat, and other popular communication tools now allow users to send messages and mails at virtually no cost, not to mention the improved efficiency they provide. Another less discussed factor of falling prices is urbanisation. Labourers migrate from rural to urban areas, which provides the manufacturing and service sectors with an abundant labour force, keeping labour cost low. China, the world's factory, with its abundant and competitive labour force, has actually helped to curb global inflation by supplying low-cost products to the global market. It is without a doubt that inflation would be a lot higher than it is today if these three factors weren't present.

When it comes to investing, it is important to take the rate of inflation into account. Let's say you deposit money in a savings account that earns 3% annually whereas the inflation rate is 5%. After a year, the nominal value of your wealth increases but your real wealth when measured in purchasing power terms actually falls. Your inflation-adjusted return is therefore a negative 2% (3% - 5% = -2%).

Stocks, precious metals, commodities and real estate are considered to be superior as a hedge against inflation. Businesses that have the ability to pass down higher raw material, labour and operating costs to consumers generally perform better and are the least affected in an inflationary environment. In addition, Treasury Inflation Protected Securities (TIPS), treasury bonds issued by the US government with its interest payment indexed to inflation, protects investors from inflation by adjusting the interest based on the Consumer Price Index (CPI) published by the government.

It is important to note that the inflation rate published by governments is the average price change measured in a basket of consumer goods across the country. Some places might have a higher inflation rate than others, even within the same nation. For instance, cities typically have a higher inflation rate than rural areas.

Inflation takes place so gradually that the average consumer usually has trouble recognising it. Some don't even notice it at all. Sir John Maynard Keynes, a distinguished English economist, was quoted saying "There is no subtler, no surer means of overturning the existing basis of society than to debauch the currency. The process engages all the hidden forces of economic law on the side of destruction, and does it in a manner which not one man in a million is able to diagnose."[163]

Hyperinflation

Technically speaking, hyperinflation occurs when prices of goods and services rise more than 50% per month over a period of time. It is a condition in which general prices increase excessively and at a rate that is out of control. Hyperinflation has happened many times in the past during wars and economic difficulties. When this took place, central banks were inclined to print massive amounts of money to finance the wars and fund government expenditures. This sudden increase in money supply fueled the first wave of inflation, causing prices to rise. Consumers, seeing the value of their cash erode, quickly ran out to spend on groceries and items that could preserve value such as gold. This loss of confidence in the monetary system exacerbated the situation and reinforced the already high inflation.

Hyperinflation wipes out the wealth of savers who keep their wealth in cash or cash equivalents. Similarly, it also wipes out the value of debts, making them easier to pay back, since a debt of the same amount can be paid back with a less valuable currency. As a response, governments around the world usually issue new currencies to replace the old ones to end the horrendous hyperinflation.

Though rare, hyperinflation has happened many times throughout history in countries such as the U.S., China, Russia, Germany and more recently, Argentina, Venezuela and Zimbabwe. Between 2007 and 2008, Zimbabwe's monthly inflation was estimated at 79.6 billion percent[164]. At that rate, it took only 24.7 hours for prices to double. When a loaf of bread cost over 10 million Zimbabwe dollars[165], it sent the majority of the population into extreme poverty. Poor billionaires were the norm in Zimbabwe. Those who saved their wealth in tangible assets, however, were able to weather the storm.

Venezuela, a South American country that possesses the world's largest proven oil reserves, is still trying to cope with hyperinflation in the present day. The International Monetary Fund (IMF) reported that Venezuela's inflation rate for 2019 was a staggering

200,000%[166]. With such a high rate of inflation, political turmoil and social unrest are commonplace. It requires more than bold leadership and fiscal discipline to restore social order and people's faith in both the government and the local currency. It is truly a test of the intelligence and patience of the policymakers.

Futures

Futures contracts are financial derivatives and legal agreements between two parties to buy or sell a particular product, usually a commodity, or a security, at a predetermined price on a specific future date. Upon the expiration date, the buyer and seller are obliged to execute the transaction, regardless of the current market price.

Futures contracts are predominantly used by big corporations to hedge against future price uncertainties. For example, fuel is a major cost in running an airline. Since airlines typically sell air tickets well in advance, and the future prices of oil are hard to predict, some major airlines choose to hedge a portion of their fuel cost by buying an oil futures contract. By doing this, the airline won't suffer higher operating costs in case oil prices spike. Similarly, a corn farmer could sell a corn futures contract to lock in the current corn prices if he believes that corn supply will increase considerably, leading to a price drop in the future.

In doing so, he is guaranteed to receive a fixed price for his corn even if its prices fall. Futures use a lot of leverage and leverage is a double-edged sword. It means that potential gains are amplified but so are potential losses. Therefore, before using a futures contract to hedge against their raw material[167], companies usually hire a financial institution such as an investment management firm to calculate the optimum number of futures contracts necessary for hedging purposes.

On the other side of the trade is usually a speculator. A speculator is a trader that speculates on the future direction of a commodity's price. Usually a hedge fund, the speculator will take a long position if they believe the price of the underlying asset or commodity will rise, or a short position if they believe the opposite.

Jeffrey Edward Gundlach, the founder of DoubleLine Capital investment firm, had established heavy short positions on the stock market before the stock market crashed in March[168]. He covered his short positions and made a fortune on the 18th of March 2020, saying, "The profits were just too great to not harvest.[169]"

In 2016, on the day U.S. president Donald Trump won the presidential election, I shorted the S&P 500 index, betting that it would crash. The market was initially volatile due to uncertainties. However, Trump quickly announced plans for a tax cut and promised to deregulate the financial market. The stock market turned around and began a parabolic rise. I turned out to be dead wrong and lost a fortune. I attribute this loss to the absence of a stop-loss order[170], something I will discuss in the next chapter.

Real Estate Investment Trust (REIT)

When it comes to real estate, most people think only of residential properties such as condos, apartments, link houses and bungalows. However, the best income-producing real estates are commercial properties such as shopping malls, retail shops, offices, hotels, warehouses, seaports, airports, hospitals, colleges and more recently, data centres. Since most investors don't have sufficient capital to purchase these commercial properties, a real estate investment trust (REIT)[171] makes it possible for small investors to invest in and collectively own the best real estates in the world. Sunway Real Estate Investment Trust (Sunway REIT), for example, owns and manages 17 properties including Sunway Putra, Sunway Tower, Sunway Pyramid Shopping Mall, Sunway University and College, and many others. Its property value has increased by over 100%[172] since it was listed on Bursa Malaysia Stock Exchange in July 2010.

REITs pay investors a steady income stream derived from rental and at the same time offer capital appreciation the way a typical real estate does. Like stocks, REITs are traded on major securities exchanges and can be bought and sold easily, therefore making them a very liquid investment vehicle. Furthermore, they are required by financial regulations to distribute 80 to 90 percent of rental incomes to investors in the form of dividend each year[173], which makes them an appropriate investment option for those who seek stability and steady income.

All REIT properties are managed professionally by a REIT manager. All that time- and labour-consuming work like renovation, looking for tenants, rent collection, property management, and repair and maintenance are all done by the REIT manager and his team. This eliminates the hassle a typical landlord faces.

Having said that, REITs do not offer leverage the way a typical real estate does. Depending on the location, you are generally required to pay a 20% down payment to purchase a property. By financing the remaining amount with a bank loan, you are actually using leverage. A little appreciation in the property value will translate into a substantial gain in relative to the initial down payment.

Another advantage of REITs is diversification. REITs enable investors to diversify and therefore reduce risks by investing in a pool of real estate assets that are located in different regions. Manulife Investment Asia Pacific REIT Fund, for instance, has investments in Singapore, Hong

Kong, Australia and other countries in the Asia Pacific region[174]. Physical property, by contrast, provides no diversification unless the investor owns a wide range of properties in different locations.

REITs are generally less volatile than stocks because company earnings fluctuate more erratically than rental incomes from properties. It is for this reason that REITs are a suitable investment for retirees and risk-averse investors.

Risk Management

Risk Management

Given that nothing is certain in the financial market, as with flying, risk management is vitally important. Risk management is the process of identifying, analysing, assessing, evaluating and controlling risks that have the potential to cause financial loss. Risks are unpredictable and can occur due to a variety of reasons such as financial market uncertainty, project failures, natural disasters, terrorist attacks, financial crises, political turmoil and social unrest, all of which are beyond the control of the average investor. While risk cannot be eliminated altogether, it can be reduced and mitigated through proper diversification, hedging, stop-loss orders and long-term holding.

Everything has risk. Despite the fact that driving incurs much greater risk than flying—causing over 1.35 million deaths worldwide every year[175], it isn't banned globally because the benefits it brings far outweigh the risk. Instead, safety features[176] and policies[177] are put in place to mitigate the risks of road accidents. As a rule, what a savvy investor does is try to obtain the maximum profit for every unit of risk taken.

Diversification

Diversification is a proper risk-management strategy. The investor reduces risk by allocating capital in a portfolio of different asset classes that have little or negative correlation. Negative correlation happens when assets move in the opposite direction. For example, stocks and bonds are known to have negative correlation. Usually, a fall in stock prices is often accompanied by a rise in bond prices. For instance, during the 2008 subprime mortgage crisis, the S&P 500 stock index crashed by over 57% whereas US treasury bonds rose aggressively, a typical reflection of capital flight from risky assets to safe haven. Moreover, of the same asset class, certain sectors tend to fall less than others. For instance, dividend stocks and utility stocks traditionally fall less than technology and growth stocks during a stock market correction. In other words, diversification works only when the securities in an investment portfolio respond to market fluctuations differently. Hence it is crucial that investors establish their own diversified portfolio based on their risk appetite, tolerance and age. Speaking of age, age does play a critical role in asset allocation. The further away an investor is from retirement, the more aggressive his or her investment should be, and therefore should tilt more towards a stock-heavy portfolio. On the contrary, a 55-year-old investor should tilt more toward a bond- and REITs-heavy portfolio. Additionally, a smart investor would diversify across different regions and currencies. As a general rule of thumb, 5 to 10 percent of a truly diversified investment portfolio should include precious metals to hedge against geopolitical risks and inflation.

Exchange traded funds (ETF) and REITs offer great diversification by investing in a wide variety of securities or properties. For example, the S&P 500 stock market index ETF (SPY) holds shares in the 500 largest capitalised corporations in the U.S. Any negative performance of one of the companies is hardly noticeable to the investor. Nonetheless, potential profits and risks go hand in hand. While minimising risk of loss, too much diversification decreases potential yields. It all boils down to whether the investor wants to eat well or sleep well.

Hedging

Apart from diversification, an investor can also use options or futures to hedge against unfavourable market movements. For a small fee, an investor can buy a put option[178] to hedge against stock market correction. Hedge funds are the pioneer and expert in hedging operations. For example, after thorough analysis and research, a hedge fund might go long the shares of a car manufacturer with a strong balance sheet and robust sales. At the same time, they might short-sell the shares of a car manufacturer that is in or about to get into financial trouble. If the auto industry as a whole has been impacted negatively by, let's say, an increase in domestic sales tax, the share price of the profitable car manufacturer should fall less than that of the troubled car manufacturer, netting a profit for the hedge fund. If, on the other hand, the government announces a lower domestic sales tax in an attempt to revive the auto industry, the share price of the profitable car manufacturer should rise more sharply than that of the troubled car manufacturer, again yielding the hedge fund a profit.

Stop-Loss Order

A stop-loss order is an order or instruction placed by the investor on the stock broker to buy or sell a security when a certain price target is hit. This technique is designed to preserve the investor's capital by cutting off any potential loss before it could happen. Suppose you invested 100 dollars in a security and placed a stop-loss order with your broker to sell when the price falls below 80 dollars. That way, you know that the maximum loss you would incur even if the market crashes severely is 20 dollars, or 20% of your investment capital.

In other words, a stop-loss order is an insurance to many risk-averse and careful investors. A stop-loss order also offers investors the peace of mind and a good night sleep. This capital-preserving trading technique allows investors to make decisions unemotionally, which is essential to successful investing. However, if the price of the security fluctuates wildly or if the asset class is generally volatile, like most commodities, a stop-loss order might not be appropriate. The price might fall and as soon as you activate your stop-loss order, it rises back up again, usually within a short time frame. For the long-term investor, though, market volatility should be used to his or her advantage and therefore a stop-loss order would not be suitable.

Holding for the Long Term

Stocks, like houses, are most likely to be profitable when they are held for a long period of time. Many financial experts recommend holding stocks for the long term to build wealth. A holding period starts when the investor purchases the stock and ends when it is sold. For the past 45 years, the S&P 500 index has experienced only 10 years of negative returns compared to 35 years of positive returns. Even if the investor bought in at the peak right before the 2008 stock market crash, and held on till the end of 2019, his investment returns would amount to 106% of his capital. For the past 100 years, the individual investor has never lost money investing in the S&P 500, provided that he or she holds on uninterrupted for 20 years[179]. As I have described earlier, short-term markets are driven by emotions, news and investors' sentiment, making them exceptionally volatile. Similarly, if you buy a house today and sell it tomorrow, the chances of you making a profit are nil. However, if you buy a house and sell it ten years later, the chances of making a profit increases significantly. Thus, a person's profit from any investment is typically proportionate to the holding period.

Human beings are emotional creatures. Many individuals claim to be long-term investors but they tend to sell when the stock market begins to fall, terrified of further losses. They then often jump back in after the market has rallied. In fact, a shrewd investor thinks of investing as grocery shopping. When something is on fire sale, during a stock market crash, for example, savvy investors cheer and look into buying stocks. They understand that stock market declines of this magnitude rarely occur and are good buying opportunities. Of course, it is possible that the market might drop further. But trying to time the market and buy at the absolute bottom is not only risky but impossible. As Peter Lynch, a well-known American investor and mutual fund manager, once said: "Far more money has been lost by investors preparing for corrections, or trying to anticipate corrections, than has been lost in corrections themselves"[180].

Chapter 3

Asset Allocation

Emerging Markets

An emerging market refers to the economy of a developing nation that is moving away from traditional economic activities[181], but has not yet achieved the status of a developed country. An emerging market economy is characterised by below average per capita income and above average gross domestic product (GDP) growth. All in all, emerging economies are in the process of transitioning from a developing to a developed economy. China and India are notably the two largest emerging economies in the world with a combined population of 2.8 billion people, which is 38% of the world's total inhabitants[182]. Other large and influential emerging economies include Brazil, Russia, Indonesia, South Korea, Mexico, Turkey, Egypt, Pakistan, Iran, Thailand and Saudi Arabia. Some less affluent emerging markets such as Vietnam, Cambodia and Myanmar are also rising rapidly.

Emerging market economies are vibrant and can offer promising returns to investors. Returns from emerging markets usually outperform that of developed countries. However, they also inhabit inherent risks such as political instability, fluctuations in commodity prices, higher mortality rates, poor infrastructures and lack of regulation. But it is important to remember that today's developed countries were once emerging nations. Hence, many investors think of emerging markets as the ticket to great wealth. Nevertheless, investors who intend to invest in emerging markets must understand the components that make up an economy and the various factors that affect economic growth.

Gross Domestic Product (GDP)

Gross domestic product (GDP) is one of the most common economic indicators used by economists to measure the productivity and track the health of a country's economy. It refers to the measure of the total market value of finished goods and services produced in an economy within a 12-month period, measured in a currency. In other words, GDP represents the level of productivity and hence, the degree of prosperity of a nation.

GDP is made up of four major components: domestic consumption, business investment, government spending and net exports (exports minus imports). Some countries, such as China and Germany who run an export-led economy, net exports constitute a large portion of the GDP. By comparison, the U.S. runs a consumer-based economy in which domestic consumption accounts for 70% of the GDP[183]. In times of recession and financial downturn, governments typically run on a budget deficit to counter the scale back in spending by individuals and corporations.

Since GDP is measured in currencies, it is subject to inflation. High inflation automatically translates into greater GDP growth, even when the overall amount of goods and services produced in the economy remains unchanged. For an overly simplified example, imagine a scenario in which you own and run a factory that manufactures shoes. Last year, the factory produced and sold 100 pairs of shoes for 10 dollars each. This year, however, due to higher raw material and operating costs, you decided to increase the selling price to 11 dollars per pair—a 10% increase in price. Like last year, you sold only 100 pairs of shoes this year, albeit at a higher price. Nonetheless, the revenue column on your spreadsheet reads 1,100 dollars, a 10% increase from last year. However, it would be a mistake if you happily inform your shareholders that your company's revenue has jumped 10% year-on-year. The fact is that the revenue, measured in the quantity of shoes sold, remained the same. As a result, to arrive at the real GDP number, you have to take inflation into consideration. Deflation, on the other hand, underreports GDP and appropriate adjustments should be made.

According to the economic data of the European Union, the rate of economic growth of an emerging market is 4% (with China and India at 7%) while that of developed economies are around 2%[184]. It means that emerging markets are growing twice as fast and this trend should continue or even accelerate, provided that the governments implement open trade policies and improve the education systems and infrastructures. Subsequently, stock markets of emerging markets might inevitably surpass that of developed nations.

I believe that investors who wish to make big bucks should put their money into investments that are about to go up, not investments that have already gone up. In this regard, investors who have at least 10 to 20 years of investment horizon should seriously consider the next rising stars: China, India and ASEAN countries.

The Rising Dragon—China

The French military genius and ruthless dictator, Napoleon Bonaparte, once famously said, "Let China sleep. For when she wakes, she will shake the world."[185]

I first visited China when I was 8 years old in 1995. I vividly remember that the streets were covered with dust, the road surfaces were uneven, and the shops along the street looked old and were in poor condition. Bicycles were the main mode of transportation and everywhere, farmers were selling their crops by the roadside. In summary, it was a typical third world country. Today, every time I fly to China, I see magnificent skyscrapers, organised cities, and German-made luxury cars on the streets. Not to mention enthusiastic business owners, first world infrastructures, and a dynamic and vibrant society.

However, from the perspective of many westerners, China is nothing more than a typical communist country. When many people think of China, they think of an authoritarian government and a closed society with no human rights or a western-style legal system. They assume anti-western and anti-capitalist sentiments, extreme poverty, and people suffering from famine and deadly diseases. Although that was true to some extent prior to Deng Xiaoping's era, anyone who has been to China recently knows that is not the case now. While China has progressed tremendously both economically and socially, most perspectives of China are still stuck in the 1950s. Perhaps the mainstream media and social media play a critical role in the formation of these perceptions.

Deng Xiaoping, the paramount leader of the People's Republic of China, famously said, "It doesn't matter whether a cat is black or white, as long as it catches mice"[186]. In 1978, he abandoned decades of ideological structures and embraced free trade policies, his actions known as "Reform and Opening"[187]. He successfully transformed a centrally planned economy to an open and free capitalist economy[188], which earned him the reputation as "Architect of Modern China"[189].

Since the Reform and Opening in 1978, China has transformed enormously from a third-world agrarian closed-society into a middle income open trade economy and industrial powerhouse. Today, China is the world's second largest economy in terms of GDP with an average economic growth rate of 9.5%[190][191]. That is remarkable by any standard. In terms of purchasing power parity (PPP), China is already the world's largest economy[192]. With a population of 1.44 billion people, China has become the world's largest market for luxury goods. Luxury goods manufacturers of fancy handbags and designer wear are sprouting up in every corner of China. Starbucks, an American multinational chain of coffeehouses, now operates more than 4,300 outlets in China alone[193].

Moreover, China is home to the world's second highest number of billionaires whose total wealth amounts to nearly 1.2 trillion dollars[194]. Of the world's top 500 largest corporations, 129 of them are headquartered in China[195]. This vast transformation has been driven by rapid industrialisation, urbanisation and globalisation, greatly influencing every aspect of its society, economy and population. I consider this astonishing economic transformation and sustained productivity growth over the past 40 years to be the miracle of the 21st century. For the first time in 2018, Hong Kong's GDP was surpassed by its neighbour Shenzhen, a high-tech and modern metropolis of China[196].

Many people have wondered about the reasons behind China's exponential growth. Now, I am not a proponent of communism myself, and what I'm about to say is descriptive and not prescriptive. In my opinion, China's success has to do with its political system. There is no election nor opposition party in China's political system and this gives the government supreme power to implement policies. Thus, efficiency is greatly improved. When not every citizen has adequate knowledge on politics and economics, but has the right to vote on policies and therefore has the ability to influence the future direction of their nation, the end results might be a less efficient system that isn't favourable to the country. For a simplified example, imagine that you are the CEO of an airline. The board of directors and you have made a decision to purchase 100 extra planes to expand the business and everyone in the airline, including the flight attendants, ground and ramp staff, guest service staff and other admin staff are to vote democratically. They are asked to share their opinions on whether the airline should purchase Boeing or Airbus planes. Considering that they have little or no knowledge about the fuel and cost efficiency, safety features and records of the two planes, the voting results will most probably be less than ideal. Ray Dalio, an American billionaire and the founder of the world's largest hedge fund, Bridgewater Associates, that manages more than 138 billion dollars worth of assets, famously stated that the best decisions are made by an idea meritocracy with believability-weighted decision making, in which the most capable and knowledgeable people's decisions, in this case, the pilots and aircraft engineers, are weighted more heavily[197].

Contrary to popular belief, more than wars and diseases, poverty has killed far more people and is likely to remain the number one killer worldwide. Based on a report released by the World Health Organization (WHO) that traced the link between health and poverty, poverty is a huge reason why babies are not vaccinated, clean water is unavailable, drugs and other treatments are in short supply, and mothers die from childbirth[198]. It has been reported that 10% of the world's population live in extreme poverty on less than 2 dollars a day[199]. Malnutrition is the leading cause of poor health and death around the world and it is the greatest challenge faced by many developing countries in Africa and the Middle East. China, in contrast, has made impressive achievements in eradicating poverty. According to the World Bank, more than 850 million Chinese people have been lifted out of extreme poverty since the economic transformation[200]. As its economy grows, its citizens climb the economic ladder and accumulate wealth, and ultimately become a burgeoning middle class.

By definition, the middle class are people and households who earn enough to satisfy their primary needs such as food, shelter, clothing, and have some disposable income left for savings, leisure and recreation. China's middle class has been the fastest growing in the world. They are hard-working adults and consumers who are the primary driver of economic growth. Moreover, in 2019 alone, more than 8.34 million Chinese students graduated from public colleges and universities in China[201]. This abundant supply of highly educated young workforce has helped China transcend its status as a manufacturing country into an innovative nation.

In 2018, China's patent applications reached 1.5 million, and accounted for 46% of patent filings globally[202].

In 2019, according to the World Intellectual Property Organisation (WIPO)[203], China surpassed the U.S. as a top source of international patent applications with 58,990 applications filed against 57,840 applications filed by the U.S.[204] Moreover, Chinese telecommunications companies are among the top in the world and account for 34% of worldwide next-generation 5G technology patent applications. As such, China is the global leader in the development of new industries that use ultrafast communications networks such as automated vehicles. Huawei Technologies, a Chinese multinational technology company, possesses the largest amount of filings for 5G at 15%[205]. It has been estimated that 5G technology will create 3.6 trillion USD in economic output and 22.3 million jobs by 2035. Therefore, its economy, and to a greater extent, its stock market, possess huge upside potential[206].

In 2017, U.K. based PricewaterhouseCoopers, a multinational professional services network of firms headquartered in London, estimated that by the year 2030, China will overtake the U.S. and become the world's largest economy with a GDP of 38.008 trillion dollars in purchasing power parity (PPP) terms[207]. Another projection by the organisation for Economic Co-operation and Development (OECD)[208], indicates that China will top the world with a GDP of 62.59 trillion dollars by 2060, with India coming second at 56.35 trillion dollars[209].

The total stock market capitalisation of China as of the first quarter of 2020 stood at around 63.97 trillion renminbi or 9.14 trillion USD[210]. With the U.S. at 35.5 trillion[211] USD, this computes a ratio of 1:3.88. In other words, the U.S. stock market valuation is 3.88 times greater than that of China. However, the nominal GDP of the U.S. was 21.44 trillion dollars in the first quarter of 2020 while China came second with a GDP of 14.14 trillion dollars[212]. That gives us a ratio of 1:1.52. In other words, U.S.'s economy is only 51.8% larger than that of China, and yet its stock market valuation is 288% greater. As you can see, China's stock market is considerably undervalued. Warren Buffett's favourite stock market indicator, the Buffett Indicator, which divides the total stock market capitalisation by the country's GDP, reveals that the U.S. stock market is extremely overvalued whereas China's is undervalued[213]. These data demonstrate that China's stock market has a lot of catching up to do.

Moreover, due to a lack of social safety nets, China has one of the world's highest savings rates. This makes the Chinese economy resilient to global economy downturns and short-term financial shocks as people still have savings to fall back on in times of financial difficulties. In addition, China also possesses the world's largest foreign exchange reserves of 3.4 trillion dollars[214], which helps with weathering global financial storms caused by adverse and volatile currency exchange rates.

Nevertheless, every country has its own problems and China is no exception. Although China is the most populous country in the world, its population is aging. According to the United Nations Population Division, based on current demographic trends, China's population will shrink from 1.44 billion in 2020 to 1.40 billion in 2050[215]. China's previous one-child policy combined with improvement in education and living standards are likely the most important contributors to this. As a result, in 2016, the Chinese government announced plans to abolish the policy and has allowed families to have two children[216]. Wages in China have risen substantially over the past two decades and thus its exports are becoming less competitive in terms of pricing. Correspondingly, the Chinese government has introduced a strategic plan, "Made in China 2025", that seeks to modernise and transform the manufacturing sector of the economy from being the world's factory manufacturing cheap and low-value goods to becoming a supplier of high-end items like semiconductors, serving industries such as aerospace and robotics[217].

China's economy is driven heavily by exports, which might render it vulnerable to geopolitical instability and the economic conditions of its trading partners. For economic growth to be sustainable and matured, its economy must shift towards domestic consumption. Moreover, its economic development is imbalanced and is currently too concentrated on the east coast, thus creating a big economic gap. As a consequence, there is income inequality between its eastern coastline megacities and less developed western inland regions. The government has acknowledged the problem and thus introduced a strategy, "Go West", to narrow the development and income gaps by investing heavily in modern infrastructure. This is to create job opportunities to better integrate the regions into the global market, as well as introduce a fairer distribution of the nation's wealth[218].

On the other side of the coin, rapid industrialisation, urbanisation and economic growth over the decades have caused immense environmental issues and pollution in China. Air pollution there has become a major threat to the public health of the Chinese. A 2015 study done by *Berkeley Earth*, a California based non-profit organisation that aims to address environmental issues such as global warming, estimated that 1.6 million Chinese die each year from lung diseases caused by polluted air[219]. Apart from industrialisation, emissions from the combustion of fossil fuels is another major anthropogenic contributor to air pollution in China. According to the *U.S. Energy Information Administration*, of the various fossil fuels, coal accounts for over 72% of the total energy needs[220]. Since 2011, China has consumed more coal than the rest of the world put together[221]. It has been estimated that China's electricity consumption will rise by 66% between 2019 and 2023[222], making pollution an ever-more challenging issue facing Chinese policymakers.

In an attempt to reduce pollution, the Chinese government has enforced stricter environmental regulations. There are also plans to reduce the reliance on coal for electricity-generation[223] and switching to renewable energies and alternative sources. In spite of being the world's largest emitter of carbon dioxide[224], China is leading the way in the world's move toward a greener economy. Since 2012, China has overtaken the U.S. as the most aggressive country in terms of investing in renewables[225] with an investment capital of 91.1 billion dollars in 2018 and 83.4 billion dollars in 2019[226]. These projects include reducing greenhouse gas and carbon dioxide emissions, developing clean and renewable energies, and encouraging and incentivising the purchase of electric vehicles. According to a report titled *The Green Economy: The Race Is On* by Deutsche Bank, China tops the world in terms of green energy investment, with 72 billion dollars spent on clean energy technology from 2000 through 2009, compared to 67 billion dollars spent by the U.S. and 38 billion dollars by Germany[227]. China already leads the way in solar and wind energy development. Research from *Solar Feeds* has projected that by year 2024, China's solar energy output will more than double that of the U.S[228]. Moreover, China is also a leader in reforestation. Between 2000 and 2010, China increased their forest coverage at an annual rate of 1.6%[229], again topping the world.

In 2013, the Chinese government adopted a global infrastructure strategy known as the "One Belt One Road" or "Belt and Road Initiative". It is an aspiring and formidable economic development strategy that focuses on building and modernising the participating countries' infrastructure and connectivity, increasing cross-border trade, and strengthening the cooperation between China, Europe, Africa and Asia. To date, more than 138 countries and 30 international organisations have participated in the project[230]. It is expected to bring enormous economic and social benefits to participating countries through improved infrastructure, greater job opportunities, increased cross-border trade, and the sharing of technology. It also has implications for the expansion and globalisation of the renminbi (RMB), which is essential if China is to become a true global superpower. If the renminbi successfully replaces the U.S. dollar and becomes the world's reserve currency, like the U.S. dollar did when it took over the

British pound in the 20th century, investments denominated in renminbi will rise in value[231].

Jim Rogers, an American billionaire investor and the co-founder of *The Quantum Fund* and *Soros Fund Management*[232] magnificently said, "The 19th century was the century of the U.K. The 20th century was the century of the U.S. The 21st century is the century of China."[233] The best way to invest in China is to buy ETFs that invest in the Chinese stock market, such as iShare MSCI China ETF (MCHI), iShare China Large Cap ETF (FXI), Xtrackers Harvest CSI 300 China A shares Fund (ASHR) and SPDR S&P China ETF (GXC). They hold a collection of Chinese stocks and thus provide diversification. As China's economy grows, its stock market should grow along with it.

The Awakening Elephant—India

Mark Twain, an American writer, entrepreneur and lecturer, said, "India is the cradle of the human race, the birthplace of human speech, the mother of history, the grandmother of legend, and the great-grandmother of tradition. Our most valuable and most artistic materials in the history of man are treasured up in India only".

Across the Himalayas to the southwest sits an enormous and populous country with more than 5,000 years of cultural history. Historically, India, along with China, was the largest economy in the world for most of the 1st through the 19th century[234]. India is the largest democracy and the second most populous country in the world with a population of 1.38 billion inhabitants[235]. They expect to surpass China this decade to become the world's most populated country. India has the best demographics of all emerging nations. Its population is young and vibrant. As of 2019, more than 53% of India's population are below the age of 30 and 68.9% are below 40[236]. Furthermore, India's fertility rate is 2.2, higher than that of China's 1.7[237]. A country needs a fertility rate of at least 2.1 to ensure that its population doesn't decline over time[238]. Japan, by sharp contrast, has a fertility rate of only 1.36[239], which if not compensated with a policy to open its borders to foreign immigrants, will face extreme challenges where less and less working adults have to support more and more retirees.

Based on numerous studies, India's labour force is expected to reach 170 million by 2020[240]. This increased labour-force participation coupled with improved educational standards will lead to greater productivity and hence better living standards. It is interesting to note that many prominent positions at global tech giants such as Google, Cisco, Microsoft, Intel and Dell are held by Indians. For example, Vinod Dham, the father of the famous Intel's Pentium microprocessor[241], comes from Pune, a sprawling city in the western Indian state of Maharashtra. These talented Indians have made significant breakthroughs in information technology and they hold prominent positions in the world of technology and communications.

The vast middle class of India will be the fuel for future economic growth. They will be both workers that contribute to the country's output and consumers that drive domestic consumption. India has a GDP of 2.94 trillion dollars[242] and is the fifth largest in the world, overtaking the U.K. and France. In the past 15 years, the Indian economy has achieved an average annual growth rate of 7.4% [243]. Moreover, India is the 3rd largest start-up base in the world with over 1,300 new start-ups in 2019 alone[244]. In addition, India is expected to have 100,000 new start-ups by 2025, which will create 3.25 million job opportunities[245]. New start-ups and small and medium enterprises (SMEs) are the backbone of an economy and account for the biggest share of a country's employment, and therefore economic development.

After independence, India began as an agrarian economy. However, over the past several decades, its manufacturing, and particularly, its service sectors, have emerged strongly. Because English is commonly spoken in India, its service sector is the fastest growing in the world and accounts for more than 60% of its economy[246]. As a result, many multinational companies base their call and service centres in India for its cheap labour cost. The drawback, however, is that service sectors generally hire less employees than manufacturing sectors do. Although they make up 60% of the economy, the service sector accounts for only 28% of national employment[247]. The Indian economy is rather unique in the sense that it has evolved from an agricultural economy to a service sector-based economy, bypassing industrialisation. Every developed nation today has gone through the process of moving from the farm to the factory and eventually to the office as their population gained skills and productivity improved.

Having said that, the long-term economic growth prospects of India remain promising and positive. Globalisation and urbanisation will continue to propel the Indian economy forward. A young population, as well as healthy savings and innovation, will likely play critical roles in shaping the country's future. In the base-case projection of Bloomberg Intelligence, India's GDP will grow from 2.7 trillion dollars in 2019 to 5 trillion dollars in 2025 and 8.4 trillion dollars by 2030[248]. This would make India's economy the third largest in the world by 2026, right behind China and the U.S. According to a study done by the International Monetary Fund (IMF), favourable demographic trends—a drop in the youth dependency ratio and longer life expectancy—should boost savings rates and allow real interest rates to fall by 150 basis points in the decade ahead[249], which should benefit economic growth by encouraging consumption and borrowing. According to a report from Boston Consulting Group (BCG), India is expected to be the third largest consumer market by 2025 with a consumer market value worth 4 trillion dollars[250]. A study conducted by PricewaterhouseCoopers estimates that India will surpass the U.S. to be the world's second largest economy in terms of purchasing power parity (PPP) by 2040[251]. It is no wonder that multinational corporations are seeking ways to expand their businesses in India.

Meanwhile, corruption has been a major problem for India's economic progress. In an attempt to eliminate corruption and reduce the use of illicit and counterfeit cash to fund illegal activities, the Indian government led by Prime Minister Narendra Modi announced plans for demonetisation in November 2016[252]. The plan was to ban all Rs 500 and Rs 1000 notes and issue new Rs 500 and Rs 2000 banknotes in exchange for the demonetised banknotes[253]. Initially, this move slowed down economic growth in certain sectors and caused great inconvenience for consumers. However, though painful in the short term, this step was necessary to rebuild the long-term health of the country's economy and restore the Indians' trust in the banking system. And it worked, because the Indians started to transfer their cash into savings accounts at an unprecedented rate instead of stashing it under the mattress. This had a positive effect on the economy as idle cash was put into the banks which was then lent out to finance productive economic activities. The plan has also been viewed by many economists as a means to a cashless India, en-route to becoming a digital society. Demonetisation has demonstrated that Indians are flexible and can easily adapt to the fast-changing world. Moreover, demonetisation has successfully reduced tax evasion by encouraging Indians to deposit their cash in banking accounts which means a rise in tax revenues for the government. According to a report from the Indian government, post-demonetisation saw an increase of 9.1 million new taxpayers, which was 80% higher than the average annual figure[254].

Another way to boost national productivity is by encouraging women to participate in the workforce. Like Japan, gender inequality in India is apparent. As the economy grows more matured and the unemployment rate falls, this huge latent workforce should be released to further propel the country's economy forward. Moreover, the ability to earn an income would put Indian women on a level playing field with their male counterparts, both socially and economically.

As with every other country, India has its own problems. Rigid labour laws, trade protectionism, populist policies, a huge income gap and gender inequality are some of the factors restricting India from achieving their economic potential. In an effort to narrow the income gap and help the agriculture sector, Prime Minister Modi approved an income support plan in 2019 to financially aid distressed farmers. Other measures that aim to improve the national productivity of the labour force have also been introduced by the Modi administration such as welfare schemes that benefit the poor. They include rural electrification, subsidies for housing and the provision of health care. Under these schemes, over 26 million households were electrified since March 2019[255]. In addition, some business-friendly policies and economic reforms have been put into effect to remove barriers to trade and ease business operations. We can expect this to improve productivity[256].

There are hundreds of languages in India and they have little similarities. For example, Hindi is the most common language, followed by Bengali, Marathi, Telugu, Tamil and others[257]. Northern Indians claim Hindi to be the country's official language whereas southern Indians view Tamil as the country's first language. The two languages are very different—many words are pronounced differently—and thus create a barrier in communication.

However, in my opinion, poor infrastructure is the most significant obstacle between India and its economic potential. To sustain continued high growth rates and become competitive in the global markets in the coming decades, India urgently needs to build reliable infrastructure, especially in transportation and power generation. It is estimated that every 1 rupee invested in infrastructure will produce more than 2 rupees in GDP, due to multiplier effects. The Indian government's ambitious programme, "Make In India"[258], that aims to level up the country's manufacturing capabilities and provide job opportunities, will have a hard time coming to fruition without proper infrastructure in place. Thus, how India will perform economically in the future depends heavily on the reforms undertaken by the government and its people.

On the 30th and 31st of July 2012, India embarrassingly experienced the largest power outage in history, affecting over 620 million people, or nearly 9% of the world's population[259]. It was later revealed that the nightmare was due to the collapse of several electrical grids that forced some power stations to go offline[260]. A power crisis of this kind was not uncommon in the past and has cost the economy a great deal. Indian politicians are well aware of the damage it has brought to the economy and has come up with plans to both enhance energy reliability and combat climate change at the same time.

As is typical with all developing economies, pollution and climate change present an uphill battle to the Indian politicians. The country has an ambitious plan to develop renewable energy to satisfy its ever-growing energy demand. India is planning to achieve 40% of its energy needs from non-fossil fuels by 2030 (currently at 30%)[261]Indian automobile maker, Tata Motors, are enthusiastic about developing electric vehicles capable of accelerating from 0 to 100 kilometres an hour under 7 seconds, not to mention a top speed of 200 kilometres an hour[262]. Among the initiatives that other governments use to combat climate change and pollution include the use of solar energy for power generation, the establishment of research institutions to develop alternative sources of energy, the regulation of green policies, and the promotion of low-carbon emission vehicles.

In summary, India should take advantage of their credible legal system, robust service-sector economy, English-speaking population, favourable demographics, and homegrown tech companies to compete in the dynamic global market.

As of the first quarter of 2020, the total market capitalisation of the S&P Bombay Stock Exchange Sensitive Index (BSE SENSEX) was about 2 trillion dollars[263]. India has a GDP of 2.94 trillion dollars[264]. On a relative basis, based on the Buffett Indicator, the Indian stock market is considered undervalued, although not as much as China's.

"If I were asked under what sky the human mind has most fully developed some of its choicest gifts, has most deeply pondered on the greatest problems of life, and has found solutions, I should point to India," said Max Mueller, a German scholar[265]. There are numerous ETFs that invest in the Indian stock market. They include: iShares MSCI India ETF (INDA), WisdomTree India Earnings Fund (EPI) and iShares India 50 ETF (INDY).

The Next European Union—ASEAN

The Association of Southeast Asia Nations (ASEAN) was established on the 8th of August 1967[266]. It is a regional intergovernmental organisation that is made up of a collective group of nations: Brunei Darussalam, Cambodia, Indonesia, Laos, Malaysia, Myanmar, the Philippines, Singapore, Thailand and Vietnam. The association aims to promote regional peace and stability, foster prosperity through unity and economic cooperation, facilitate cross-border trade, and provide assistance to member countries in need.

Together, they cover a total land area of more than 1.7 million square miles, have a combined population of over 650 million and a nominal GDP of 2.8 trillion dollars[267].

Unlike the European Union, ASEAN countries have high birth rates. Between 1980 and 2018, their population nearly doubled, increasing from 355 million to 649 million. Moreover, the population structure indicates that the share of the youth population represents 34% of the total population. In addition, its working age population (people aged 15 to 59) increased from 61.4% in 2000 to 61.8% in 2018[268].

Education is an important contributor to economic growth because equipping the population with better knowledge and skills will improve their productivity. Over the past few decades, the adult literacy rate of the member countries has improved significantly, averaging above 90%[269]. It is not hard to imagine that in the not too distant future, the productivity of the population will exceed that of their western counterparts. This, coupled with efficient allocation of capital and resources, and the rise of its middle class, will undoubtedly make ASEAN an important global economy player in the 21st century. In 2019, ASEAN's GDP grew at 4.8%, higher than the growth rate of 3% of the global economy[270] and more than double the growth rate achieved by the U.S.'s 2.3%[271]. It is estimated that the total GDP of ASEAN will reach 10 trillion dollars by 2030[272]. That is over 3 times greater than its GDP today and hence represents huge investment opportunities for global investors.

In 2019, among the ASEAN countries, Cambodia, Laos and Vietnam[273] had despite global political tensions and geopolitical risks achieved GDP growth rates of 7%, 6.8% and 6.5% respectively[274].

Vietnam's economic development and progress over the past few decades have been impressive. Despite being a communist country, the government abandoned old-fashioned closed society and centrally planned economic policies. In its place, they adopted economic reforms similar to those adopted by their neighbour China. Since then, its GDP per capita has increased dramatically to reach 2,700 dollars in 2019[275]. Its poverty rate has declined significantly from over 70% to below 6%. That was a remarkable achievement. Its export-led economy is growing fast, earning it the title "The second China". Moreover, with a population of 97.3 million people with rising wealth and income, it is set to be a big consumer market for multinationals. Today, motorcycles are still the primary means of transportation, but it won't last that way for long. It is no wonder that international giant car makers such as Toyota are planning to expand their business territory in the Vietnamese market. Furthermore, in May 2020, Politico[276] ranked Vietnam No.1 in the world in fighting the Covid-19 pandemic[277]. This shows the superior efficiency of its government and cooperation of its citizens.

Cambodia, another fast-growing emerging economy, has a population of 16.7 million and a GDP of 27.1 billion dollars[278]. Over the past two decades, Cambodia's economy managed to grow at an average rate of 8%, one of the highest in the region[279]. The last time I flew to Phnom Penh, the capital city of Cambodia, I saw a high number of used cars on the road. The road traffic in the major cities are getting more congested, a symbol of a vigorous economy. Political stability and economic reforms should continue to keep its economic growth sustainable.

Indonesia, the world's largest Islamic country located in the southern part of the region, is the fourth most populous country in the world with a population of 273.8 million people[280]. It has a GDP of 1.02 trillion dollars, the largest among the ASEAN countries[281]. The country is rapidly going through the industrialisation process and has the potential to become an economic powerhouse in the region. The International Monetary Fund (IMF) has estimated that by 2030, Indonesia will have a GDP of 10.1 trillion dollars in purchasing power parity (PPP) terms, making it the fourth largest economy in the world, right behind the U.S.[282] I have been to Indonesia numerous times before and have noticed that the people are hardworking, intelligent and have a strong desire for a higher standard of living. However, Indonesia is also located in the world's most natural disaster-prone region where earthquakes, volcanic eruptions and landslides occur frequently. Moreover, the country comprises a total of 17,508 islands, making it relatively hard to manage[283].

The Philippines is a country located in the western Pacific Ocean. It has a population of 109.7 million people[284] and a GDP of 330.9 billion dollars[285]. Like Indonesia, it consists of many islands: 7,641 in total[286]. It was once the wealthiest nation in the region. But ever since the President Marcos era, the Philippines's economy has declined sharply due to immense corruption. Today, it is the world's largest exporter of maids. It would take bold and strong leadership to steer the country back on the right track. Since President Rodrigo Duterte came in power, a lot of changes have taken place. The most notable policies under his leadership are the war on drugs and anti-terrorism act. Being a U.S. colony in the past, its infrastructures are relatively well-maintained compared to other ASEAN countries. I am certain that the Philippines will one day regain its glory and prosper economically.

Brunei is a relatively small country when compared to the other ASEAN countries. It is surrounded by the South China Sea on the north and Malaysia's state of Sarawak on the south. It has a population of only 438,000 people, making it the smallest economy in the region[287]. Brunei has a large amount of proven oil reserves and this makes it one of the richest countries in the world in terms of national wealth per capita. Because of its enormous oil revenues, Brunei is one of the few countries that doesn't levy income tax on its citizens. This tax advantage works in the favour of domestic consumption because more disposable income means higher purchasing power. However, over-reliance on oil revenues make Brunei vulnerable to the volatility of international crude oil prices. Nonetheless, economic reforms and diversification should provide a second growth engine for the economy.

Thailand, a popular tourist destination, has a population of 69.8 million people[288]. It is the second largest economy in Southeast Asia with a GDP of 504.9 billion dollars[289]. Thailand is a newly industrialised economy. Many multinational corporations such as Honda and Toyota have set up manufacturing bases in the country. Tourism is an important sector of the economy too and accounts for over 5.65% of its GDP[290]. Bangkok, Phuket, Krabi, and Chiangmai are examples of popular tourist destinations in Thailand. However, the export-led economy and heavy reliance on tourism makes Thailand vulnerable to global economic downturns. For example, the Covid-19 outbreak in the first quarter of 2020 has severely impacted the tourism industry and the country's economy. In June 2020, the Thai government announced a plan for relaxed measures for foreigners entering Thailand in a desperate attempt to kick start the tourism industry[291]. Although the situation following the pandemic might seem bleak, it will eventually turn around and the country will prosper once again. It is important to note that Thailand is the only country in Southeast Asia that has never been colonised by European or Japanese powers. This reflects the high intelligence and unity of the Thai people and their leaders.

Laos is an inland country bordered by China, Thailand, Vietnam, Cambodia and Myanmar. It has a population of 7.29 million people[292] and a GDP of 18.1 billion dollars[293]. Laos is a fast-growing middle-income economy. With the knowledge that the country lacks capital and resources to grow and compete with its neighbours, the government has adopted several open trade economic policies and enacted laws and regulations to enhance private ownership of properties and businesses. In recent years, the country saw a dramatic surge in foreign direct investment (FDI), especially from China. These policies are similar to those adopted by China in the 1980s and 1990s, which have helped create job opportunities and stimulated economic growth. However, Laos faces unique challenges as the country is surrounded by land, which makes exports and imports not only inefficient but also highly costly. Thus, the cost of living in Laos is relatively high compared to its neighbouring countries. Even usual household goods and food, such as eggs and chicken, are imported from Thailand. Developing the agriculture sector should be an urgent agenda for the current administration. In fact, Laos is very similar to Switzerland in that both nations are mountainous and have limited land and population. Therefore, Laos could adopt economic strategies similar to that of Switzerland by developing the country into a regional financial hub. They could also focus on precision manufacturing of high value-added goods such as medical and aerospace equipment. Nevertheless, this requires talent and hence, the administration must come up with a programme with generous incentives to attract oversea talents.

Myanmar is an emerging market that is rich in oil, natural gas, jade and other mineral resources. It has a population of 54.45 million people[294] and a GDP of 68.7 billion dollars[295]. Like Laos, Myanmar has seen its foreign direct investment (FDI) surge dramatically in recent years, and it has contributed to economic development. Unlike Thailand and Vietnam, Myanmar is relatively slow in economic transformation. It is still an agriculture-based economy due to their lack of skilled laborers and basic infrastructure. However, the country's enormous oil and natural gas reserves could be a turning point for its economy and people. Policymakers should attract foreign oil companies to extract oil and build oil refineries in the country by offering favourable incentives, as well as enacting laws to protect private property ownership. My dad has many Myanmarese workers on the payroll at his factory and I can tell you that they are both smart and hardworking. I was stunned when I discovered that they'd learned basic Bahasa Malaysia, the national language of Malaysia, within two weeks! Having said that, political instability continues to cast a shadow over the country's economic development. Finding a sustainable solution to the problem should be the government's number one priority.

Singapore, the home to many of the world's best—world's best airport, world's best airline, world's most competitive economy, world's best country in doing business and so forth—has a population of 5.86 million people[296] and a GDP of 372 billion dollars[297]. Under the leadership of Lee Kuan Yew, the former prime minister of Singapore, the tiny country successfully transformed itself from a third world into a first world nation. Situated south of the Malay peninsula, Singapore is also the only advanced country in the region with one of the world's highest GDP per capita at 65,977 dollars[298]. Singapore was initially part of the new federation of Malaysia, along with Malaya, Sabah and Sarawak. Political differences created conflicts that eventually led to the departure of the country from the federation. They subsequently became an independent country. Rapid industrialisation and financialisation between the 1960s and 1990s earned

Singapore the title "The Four Little Dragons"[299], along with Hong Kong, Taiwan and South Korea. Knowing that the country lacks arable land and natural resources, the government has relied exclusively on economic strategies to promote free trade and encourage entrepreneurship. As a consequence, they have successfully established Singapore as a global financial hub and major trading port. Moreover, to counter the adverse effect of population decline, the government implemented a viable immigration policy to attract global talents. To maintain its prosperity and global competitiveness, though, Singapore will have to cooperate closely with its neighbouring countries in this challenging 21st century.

Last but not least, Malaysia, the country I live and grew up in, consists of Peninsular Malaysia (West Malaysia) and Borneo's East Malaysia. It has a population of 32.4 million people[300] and a GDP of 358.6 billion dollars[301]. After gaining independence from the U.K. in 1957, its economy has grown at an average annual rate of 6.32% since 1961[302]. Malaysia is a multiethnic country, which has a significant impact on its politics. Behind Singapore and Brunei, Malaysia's newly industrialised export-oriented market economy has enabled its people to enjoy a lifestyle comparable to that of many developed western countries. Under the economic transformation programme promoted by the Malaysian government, the country has successfully transformed into a middle-income industrialised country and has become an important global supplier of semiconductors and electronics. However, the country's economic development is imbalanced. Too much weight and emphasis have been placed on developing West Malaysia, particularly its capital city, Kuala Lumpur, while leaving East Malaysia far behind in terms of productivity and spending power. A balanced market economy is essential to sustain its high economic growth and ensure racial unity. Malaysia is a blessed country where there are no earthquakes, volcanos, typhoons or other natural disasters. With proper structural and economic reforms, elimination of corruption, improvement in education system, and bold and determined leadership, Malaysia is set to escape the middle-income trap and achieve *Wawasan Kemakmuran Bersama 2030* (Shared Prosperity Vision 2030) to become a wealthy nation.

All in all, the ASEAN countries have a total population of 650 million people and a combined GDP of 2.8 trillion dollars. Therefore, its potential should not be underestimated. These vibrant and dynamic economies are expected to grow at rates much faster than that of the western world and is likely to be a major contributor to global economic growth. There were even talks of a single common currency, similar to the euro, within ASEAN.

However, lessons of the European sovereign debt crisis from the first decade of the 21st century have shifted their focus to economic cooperation instead. Afterall, giving up sovereignty by letting a foreign central bank set interest rates and decide on monetary policies is a recipe for failure.

Investors who wish to invest in ASEAN can buy Global X FTSE ASEAN 40 ETF (ASEA), an ETF that invests in some of the best publicly traded companies in ASEAN.

Conclusion

We are living in fascinating times because we get to witness the great transfer of wealth and power from the west to the east. Based on an analysis from PricewaterhouseCoopers, by 2040, the total economic output of the E7 (China, India, Indonesia, Brazil, Russia, Mexico and Turkey) could be double that of the G7 (the U.S., the U.K., France, Germany, Japan, Canada and Italy)[303]. Investing successfully means putting money in investments where the upside potential greatly outweighs the risks. When you invest or spend the cash that would otherwise be sitting idly in a bank account, even a very small portion of it, you are literally putting it to constructive use by contributing to the growth of the economy (recall that domestic consumption and investment are two important components of GDP). By investing in the stock market, you are actually providing capital to companies which will in turn use the capital to set up new plants, hire people, buy new equipment, and fund research and developments. All of these will result in a better economy and lower unemployment, which are the basis of a stable and prosperous society. It is important to remember that today's developed countries were once emerging nations.

Another way to benefit from the rise of the emerging markets is to invest in companies that have large business exposure in these nations. For instance, multinationals such as Apple (AAPL), Johnson & Johnson (JNJ), Procter & Gamble (PG) and Boeing (BA) derive a big portion of their revenues from emerging markets. As the people in developing countries get richer and propensity to spend becomes greater, their contribution to the bottom lines of these multinationals should increase. Nevertheless, a lot has to be done before they can achieve their full potential, such as economic and structural reforms, elimination of corruption and trade protectionism. Furthermore, they could benefit from improved infrastructure and education systems, free trade policies, modern technologies, enactment of rules of law, and the list goes on. Otherwise, potential will remain as just potential. Only time will tell if China, India and the ASEAN dreams will materialise. How the future will unfold remains to be seen. However, if you are a long-term investor, time is on your side.

<u>Acknowledgements</u>

I would never have written this book if I did not get the wonderful opportunity to fly around the world, which has broadened my horizon in extraordinary ways . For that, I would like to thank my company, AirAsia, for offering me a career as a pilot, not to mention great opportunities to meet exciting people and travel to beautiful places.

I would also like to acknowledge those who encouraged me to write this book. To my colleagues and bosses at AirAsia, for being encouraging and motivating, as well as supportive of me as I wrote this book. I remain grateful for their support, many of whom have inspired and influenced me over the years. I should say a special thanks to all my flight instructors, all of whom inspired me to not just be a competent pilot, but also a responsible human being.

I am indebted to my co-author, Ceci Pong Pui See, for her excellent work and thrilling experiences and stories, of which she shares with us during the second part of this book. I also thank her for the many weekends she had to give up to write the book. When I first thought of writing this book and was in search of a co-author to write the portion on the cabin crew experience, she was the first person that popped into my mind. Her work makes this book complete.

I must also thank Capt. Lee Chow Ping, the editor of this book, for her exceptional skills in editing my initial manuscript. She has provided valuable information on many of the legal aspects of publishing this book.

Thanks too to Ng Suen Yi, a professional graphic designer, for designing the cover of this book. Her work makes the book look captivating and appealing.

Last but not least, thank you to my family for their unconditional support and love.

We have tried hard to correct the mistakes and errors in the book. Nonetheless, any errors that remain are my sole responsibility.

Lim Kok Kean

October
2020

About the Author

Howard Lim Kok Kean is a captain at AirAsia Berhad. He flies the Airbus 320 and has accumulated close to 10,000 flying hours. He is also a part-time licenced investment adviser at Kenanga Investors Berhad, a Malaysian financial services firm.

Howard loves reading, especially about finance and economics. At the age of 31, he earned his investment adviser's licence issued by the Federation of Investment Managers Malaysia (FIMM). Present day, he helps his clients plan and achieve their financial goals.

He lives in Kuala Lumpur with his family.

About the Co-Author

Ceci Pong Pui See is a simple girl from a small town. She began her flying career with AirAsia and AirAsia X. As a former senior cabin crew for AirAsia, she has experience on the Airbus 320 and Airbus 330. She eventually decided to join Singapore Airlines, not only to achieve a better life for her family but also to explore and progress in her flying career. In Singapore Airlines, she was rated on the Airbus 330, Airbus 350, Airbus 380 and Boeing 777. On top of that, she was trained for Business Class and is equipped to provide the finest personal service for the enjoyment and comfort of her passengers.

Present day, Ceci is an instructor with CAE, a training centre that provides training for various roles in the aviation industry. She is well-versed in fast-paced environments, thanks to more than 10 years of accumulated experience in the aviation industry and customer relations. She has worked with a wide range of clientele as building long-term relationships is what she does best. Her ability to provide cutting-edge solutions has made her a valuable member to have on a team.

Besides that, she is also qualified as a trainer by PSMB Malaysia and has successfully passed the examination for Dangerous Goods Regulations Cat 6 by DGM Support Malaysia. She has experience in SAREX LIMA'19 Land and Sea Training and survival training with SMART NADMA'19.

She is grateful for the series of events that has led her to this point in life and will continue to learn with a kind and humble heart.

Endnotes

Preface

1. Aurelio Locsin, "Is Air Travel Safer Than Car Travel?" *USA Today,* n.d., https://traveltips.usatoday.com/air-travel-safer-car-travel-1581.html.
2. Abdul Kareem, "Review of Global Menace of Road Accidents With Special Reference to Malaysia - A Social Perspective," *Malaysian Journal of Medical Sciences,* 10, no. 2, (2003), http://journal.usm.my/journal/MJMS-10-2-031.pdf.
3. International Civil Aviation Organisation—a specialised agency of the United Nations that governs, regulates promotes and fosters the safety, planning and development of international civil aviation.
4. "Accident Statistics," *ICAO,* n.d., https://www.icao.int/safety/iStars/Pages/Accident-Statistics.aspx
5. CAE is a global leader in civil aviation training, defence and security, and healthcare; founded in 1947.
6. "World's Best Low-Cost Airlines 2019," *Skytrax World Airline Awards,* 2019, https://www.worldairlineawards.com/worlds-best-low-cost-airlines-2019/.
7. "2018 World Airline Awards Results Announced," *Skytrax World Airline Awards,* July 17, 2018, https://www.worldairlineawards.com/2018-world-airline-awards-results-announced/.

Part One: Inside the Cockpit

Taking to the Sky

8. On October 22nd.
9. William Rankin, "MEDA Investigation Process," *Boeing,* n.d., https://www.boeing.com/commercial/aeromagazine/articles/qtr_2_07/AERO_Q207_article3.pdf.
10. Diane Tedeschi, "Crash in the Canary Islands," *Air & Space,* June 2019, https://www.airspacemag.com/history-of-flight/reviews-crash-in-canary-islands-180972227/.
11. Both domestic and international.
12. "Domestic and International Tourist Arrivals to Langkawi District," *Langkawi Municipal Council,* n.d., http://www.mplbp.gov.my/en/citizens/services/tourism/page/0/1.
13. The largest show of its kind within the Asia Pacific Region.
14. Single-engine and twin-engine respectively.

Joining the Airline

15. S&P 500 is a stock market index that represents the 500 largest U.S. publicly traded companies by market capitalisation.
16. Manoj Singh, "The 2007-08 Financial Crisis in Review," *Investopedia*, July 26, 2020, https://www.investopedia.com/articles/economics/09/financial-crisis-review.asp.
17. Printing money to buy financial assets.
18. A stock market index that comprises the 30 largest public companies by full market capitalisation.
19. Joseph Chin, "Disappointing 2008 With KLCI Losing Nearly 39% Amid Global Crisis," *The Star*, January 1, 2009, https://www.thestar.com.my/business/business-news/2009/01/01/disappointing-2008-with-klci-losing-nearly-39-amid-global-crisis.
20. Le Bourget, "AirAsia Wins 11th Consecutive World's Best Low-Cost Airline Award at Skytrax," *AirAsia*, June 18, 2019, https://newsroom.airasia.com/news/airasia-wins-11th-consecutive-worlds-best-low-cost-airline-award-at-skytrax.
21. A popular tourist attraction in Kuala Lumpur.
22. Inventor of the lightbulb.
23. When an airliner flies from one airport to another, it goes through different airspaces. Different airspaces use different radio frequencies.
24. An alternate airport is a second option to which an aircraft may proceed if the original airport of arrival is found to be unsuitable for landing, may it be due to weather or downgraded equipment.
25. A Parking Checklist is performed to ensure that the aircraft is properly shut down, the external lights are set, the parking brake set, etc.

How to Become a Pilot

26. Formerly known as the Department of Civil Aviation (DCA), CAAM is the government agency and regulatory body under the Ministry of Transport (MOT) that regulates the safety and security, as well as ensures efficient management of civil aviation in Malaysia.
27. "Medical Requirement," *CAAM*, April 2019, https://www.caam.gov.my/wp-content/uploads/Medical-Requirement-Issue-2-Amendment-1.pdf.
28. Ibid.
29. Due to a variety of factors such as poor health conditions and medication.
30. "A320, Vicinity Abu Dhabi UAE, 2012," *Skybrary*, Last Edited December 6, 2018, https://www.skybrary.aero/index.php/A320,_vicinity_Abu_Dhabi_UAE,_2012.
31. "ELP Provisions," *CAAM*, February 24, 2015, https://www.caam.gov.my/sectors-divisions/air-traffic-inspectorate/elp-provisions/.
32. Kenneth J. Cooper, "At Least 349 Are Killed in Collision," *Washington Post*, November 13, 1996, http://www.washingtonpost.com.

33. "AirAsia Cadet Pilot Programme (2019)," *Better Aviation*, 2019, https://betteraviationjobs.com/job/airasia-cadet-pilot-2019/.

34. "CPL (Commercial Pilot's Licence,)" *Malaysian Flying Academy*, n.d., https://www.mfa.edu.my/courses/cpl-commercial-pilot's-licence-synopsis.

35. "From Ground to Sky - Part 2," *Malaysian Flying Academy*, n.d., https://www.mfa.edu.my.

36. A set of rules that govern flights under visual meteorological conditions (VMC) in which flying is based solely on visual references.

37. A set of rules that govern flights under instrument meteorological conditions (IMC) in which flights are conducted based on instruments in the cockpit without any outside references.

38. A solo flight is when the student flies alone without the presence of an instructor.

39. "Road Safety Annual Report 2019," *International Transport Forum*, 2019, https://www.itf-oecd.org/sites/default/files/germany-road-safety.pdf.

40. "Driving in Germany," *The German Way & More*, n.d., https://www.german-way.com/travel-and-tourism/driving-in-europe/driving/.

41. "AirAsia Cadet Pilot Programme (2019)," *Better Aviation*, 2019, https://betteraviationjobs.com/job/airasia-cadet-pilot-2019/.

42. The MPL training course aims to train student pilots to operate as a co-pilot in a multi-engine, multi-pilot commercial aircraft. CPL, on the other hand, is a flying licence that enables the holder to act as the pilot of an aircraft and get paid for his or her work. A CPL holder is permitted to fly solo in a private plane and act as a pilot in a commercial jet whereas an MPL holder is only permitted to fly as a co-pilot in a multi-pilot airplane.

43. Scott Shappell et al., "Human Error and Commercial Aviation Accidents," *Federal Aviation Administration*, July 2006, https://www.faa.gov.

Inside the Cockpit

44. Mike Kopp, "Pilot Uniforms," *Jetlinx*, n.d., https://www.jetlinx.com/from-the-flight-deck-pilot-uniforms/.

45. "Pan American World Airways, Inc.," *Britannica*, n.d., https://www.britannica.com/topic/Pan-American-World-Airways-Inc.

46. Nicholas Cummins, "China Is a Driving Factor Behind the World's Pilot Shortage," *Simple Flying*, October 25, 2018, https://simpleflying.com/china-is-a-driving-factor-behind-the-worlds-pilot-shortage/.

47. Jethro Mullen, "Want to Earn $300,000 Tax Free? Try Flying a Plane in China," *CNN Money*, November 15, 2015, https://money.cnn.com/2016/11/15/news/economy/china-airlines-foreign-pilots-pay/index.html.

48. "Developing Countries and Emerging Markets," *European Commission*, n.d., https://ec.europa.eu/knowledge4policy/foresight/topic/growing-consumerism/developing-countries-emerging-markets_en.

49. "ASEAN Growth Slower Than Forecasted," *The Asean Post*, December 30, 2019, https://theaseanpost.com/article/asean-growth-slower-forecasted.

50. "GDP Growth (Annual %)," *The World Bank*, n.d., https://data.worldbank.org.

51. The PIC may choose to reject an aircraft if it is not up to his or her standard.

52. It usually takes longer on a wide-body aircraft.

53. "AirAsia Malaysia Based Captain," *Better Aviation,* n.d., https://betteraviationjobs.com/job/airasia-captain-base-in-malaysia-april-2015/.

54. "Flight Time (FTL) and Flight Duty Period (FDP) Limitations," *CAAM,* December 1, 2005, https://aip.caam.gov.my.

55. If the hours are evenly distributed throughout a 12-month period.

56. E.g. the airport and enroute navigational charts.

57. A NOTAM is a notice that contains information essential to the operation of a flight that is not known far enough in advance to be published by other means.

58. A SNOWTAM is a notice describing the conditions of the runways, taxiways and apron of an airfield. It is issued when the runway is contaminated with standing water, slush, snow or ice.

59. During poor weather conditions, air traffic control may increase the separation between flights.

60. Fuel, water or hydraulic leaks are all possible scenarios.

61. Such as flaps, ailerons and rudders.

62. Such as baggage loading, refuelling, refilling of water, waste drainage, and deicing and anti-icing procedures.

63. Harro Ranter, "Accident Description," *Aviation Safety Network,* n.d., https://aviation-safety.net.

64. As well as its certifications.

65. An FMGS is a specialised complex automation system that performs a variety of in-flight tasks that aims to reduce the workload of pilots and at the same time provide accurate data and predictions to enhance the pilots' situational awareness.

66. The pilots will total the weight of the aircraft, its equipment, the passengers, payload and uplifted fuel to determine the take-off weight. With this weight, they would calculate the ground speed at which the aircraft lifts off the runway.

67. This is typically done by the pilot that would be operating the sector. It includes a rejected take-off brief and a departure brief.

68. "Aircraft Accident Report," *FAA,* n.d., https://lessonslearned.faa.gov.

69. "Eight Killed In Plane Crash," *TVNZ,* July 6, 2003, https://tvnz.co.nz.

70. Slats and flaps are high-lift devices used during take-off to generate greater lift by increasing the wing surface area and shape.

71. A long flight would cover a longer ground distance and therefore it is more economical to fly at higher altitudes since air density is lower at higher altitudes, so this reduces drag and improves fuel efficiency. On the other hand, a short flight covers a shorter ground distance, where the top of the climb is quickly followed by the top of descent, making higher level cruise impractical.

72. "All Engines-Out Landing Due to Fuel Exhaustion, Air Transat, Airbus A1330-243 Marks C-G9TS, Lajes, Azores, Portugal, 24 August 2001," October 18, 2004, http://www.fss.aero/accident-reports/dvdfiles/PT/2001-08-24-PT.pdf.

73. This typically includes the approach speed and landing distance.

74. David Carbaugh, *Aero Magazine,* Issue 19, n.d., http://www.boeing.com/commercial/aeromagazine/aero_19/approach_story.html

75. Ibid.

76. Or if visibility is below the airfield's limitations.

77. GPWS is a system designed to alert pilots when the aircraft is approaching terrain.

78. Harro Ranter, "Accident Description," *Aviation Safety Network*, n.d., https://aviation-safety.net/database/record.php?id=19920731-0

79. Sabrina Houston, "The I'M SAFE Checklist," *The Balance Careers*, November 20, 2019, https://www.thebalancecareers.com/the-i-m-safe-checklist-282948.

80. "CLEAR," *Aviation Knowledge*, Last Edited September 7, 2012, http://aviationknowledge.wikidot.com/aviation:clear.

81. "Threat and Error Management (TEM)," *Skybrary*, Last Edited August 4, 2017, https://www.skybrary.aero/index.php/Threat_and_Error_Management_(TEM).

82. Chip Wright, "Verbalise, Verify, Monitor," *AOPA*, May 10, 2017, https://blog.aopa.org/aopa/2017/05/10/verbalize-verify-monitor/.

83. The crash in Stonycreek Township killed nearly 3,000 people.

84. "Chapter 1.1: 'We Have Some Planes': Inside the Four Flights," *9/11 Commission Report. National Commission on Terrorist Attacks Upon the United States*, 2004, https://www.9-11commission.gov/report/911Report_Ch1.pdf

85. "Colonel Gaddafi 'Ordered Lockerbie Bombing'," *BBC News*, February 23, 2011, https://www.bbc.com/news/uk-scotland-south-scotland-12552587.

86. Ahmad Fairuz Othman, Adib Povera and Sarah Rahim, "Cyberattack Hits KLIA, KLIA2?" *New Straits Times*, August 24, 2019, cyberattack-hits-klia-klia2.

87. "Safety Management Systems (SMS) for Civil Aviation," *IATA*, n.d., https://www.iata.org/en/training/courses/sms-civil-aviation/tals03/en/.

Misconceptions About Flying

88. Take-off and landing are the most critical phases of flight.

89. Claudia Cuskelly, "Flight Secrets REVEALED: Why Cabin Crew Have Just 90 Seconds to Evacuate in an Emergency," *Express*, September 6, 2017, https://www.express.co.uk/travel/articles/850701/flight-secrets-cabin-crew-emergency-evacuation-time.

90. Joseph Trevithick, "Russia Releases Terrifying Video of Superjet Airliner Drifting to a Stop in a Ball of Flames," *The Drive*, April 15, 2020, https://www.thedrive.com/the-war-zone/33030/russia-releases-terrifying-video-of-superjet-airliner-drifting-to-a-stop-in-a-ball-of-flames.

91. "Terms and Conditions of Carriage for AK Flights," *AirAsia*, n.d., https://www.airasia.com.

92. Lauren Mack, "Air Travel and Pregnancy," *Cheapflights*, November 9, 2017, https://www.cheapflights.com/news/air-travel-and-pregnancy.

93. Salil Deshpande, "Do Babies Born on Airplanes Get Visa-Free Travel Across the World?", *Conde Nast Traveller*, February 20, 2019, https://www.cntraveller.in/story/explained-happens-baby-born-airplane.

94. In both scenarios, the pilots will need to perform take-off, climb, cruise, descent, approach and landing.

95. "Road Traffic Injuries," *World Health Organisation*, February 7, 2020, https://www.who.int/news-room/fact-sheets/detail/road-traffic-injuries

96. Although larger aircraft might tend to have more redundancies.

97. Abby Tang and Clancy Morgan, "It's Physically Impossible To Open an airplane Door Mid-Flight. Here's Why," *Business Insider*, https://www.businessinsider.com/why-plane-doors-cant-open-mid-flight-2020-2.

98. Gary Leff, "Why Do HEPA Air Filters Protect Us from Covid-19 on Planes?" *View From the Wing*, *why-do-hepa-air-filters-protect-us-from-covid-19-on-planes*.

99. Edward J. Rupke, "What Happens When Lightning Strikes an Airplane," *Scientific American*, August 14, 2006, https://www.scientificamerican.com/article/what-happens-when-lightni.

100. Kelsey Munro, "How Safe Is Flying? Here's What the Statistics Say," *SBS News*, Updated July 31, 2018, https://www.sbs.com.au/news/how-safe-is-flying-here-s-what-the-statistics-say.

101. "Aviation Benefits Report," *ICAO*, 2019, https://www.icao.int/sustainability/Documents/AVIATION-BENEFITS-2019-web.pdf.

102. Kelsey Munro, "How Safe Is Flying? Here's What the Statistics Say," *SBS News*, Updated July 31, 2018, https://www.sbs.com.au/news/how-safe-is-flying-here-s-what-the-statistics-say.

103. "Air Benefits Report," *ICAO*, 2019, https://www.icao.int/sustainability/Documents/AVIATION-BENEFITS-2019-web.pdf.

104. Maggie Teneva, "10 Common Reasons for Flight Delays," *Sky Refund*, n.d., https://skyrefund.com/en/blog/ten-reasons-for-flight-delays.

105. "Aviation Benefits Report," *ICAO*, 2019, https://www.icao.int/sustainability/Documents/AVIATION-BENEFITS-2019-web.pdf

106. "Auditing Annex 17 Standards," *ICAO*, October 2018, https://www.icao.int.

107. Radar vector is when ATC uses a flight radar to guide the pilots, giving them instructions like altitude, heading or speed to fly.

108. A situation in which a layer of water separates and builds between the aircraft's tyres and the runway surface.

Part Two: Inside the Cabin

Shine and Soar

109. "AirAsia Berhad Annual Report 2009," *AirAsia*, 2009, https://ir.airasia.com/misc/ar2009.pdf.

110. Ibid.

111. Ibid.

112. "What's Your Career Destination?" *AirAsia*, n.d., https://careers.airasia.com.

113. It is important to understand the background, culture and values of your company.

114. To understand the features of the aircraft you are going to operate.

115. There is a lot of terminology in aviation, and the cabin crew are required to have basic understanding of these aviation terms.

116. BLS—Basic Life Support Training such as CPR (cardiopulmonary resuscitation) etc.

117. Crashland and water drill; smoke and fire drill etc.

118. Manage disruptive passengers onboard.

119. To create awareness among able-bodied people as well as empower disabled people.

120. To understand the calculation of Flight Duty Limitations.

121. A crew is said to be "operating solo" when he or she does so with minimum or no guidance.

122. AirAsia aircraft are mostly painted red.

123. AirAsia X is a low-cost airline based in Kuala Lumpur.

124. "AirAsia X's Maiden Flight to Gold Coast," *The Star*, September 29, 2007, https://www.thestar.com.my/news/nation/2007/09/29/airasia-xs-maiden-flight-to-gold-coast.

125. Nina Ruggiero, "Why Singapore Airlines Was Voted the Best International Airline 25 Years in a Row," *Travel and Leisure*, July 8, 2020, https://www.travelandleisure.com/worlds-best/singapore-airlines-best-international-airline-25-years.

126. "Cabin Crew," *Singapore Airlines*, n.d., https://www.singaporeair.com/en_UK/us/careers/cabin-crew-career/.

127. Ibid.

128. For experienced cabin crew, you may also bring your relevant training certificates from your previous airline.

129. A copy of personal identification card, passport, etc.

130. "Cabin Crew," *Singapore Airlines*, n.d., https://www.singaporeair.com/en_UK/us/careers/cabin-crew-career/.

131. The IATA code of Singapore Airlines.

132. Just like AirAsia, we were required to operate 3 supernumerary flights, then fly normal line flights under supervision for 6 months (probation period).

133. Air Sommelier is a rigorous wine programme. Certain staff members attain Level 2, then Level 3 certification from the internationally recognised Wine and Spirit Education Trust (WSET)—along with an in-house training programme to be designated an "Air Sommelier".

134. "World's Best Airline Cabin Crew 2019," *Skytrax World Airline Awards*, 2019, https://www.worldairlineawards.com/worlds-best-airline-cabin-crew-2019/.

135. CAE is a worldwide leader of training in civil aviation, defence and security, and healthcare.

136. "CAE Kuala Lumpur," *CAE*, n.d., https://www.cae.com/civil-aviation/locations/cae-kuala-lumpur.

137. Ibid.

<u>My Aviation Experience</u>

138. Flights where we operate back not long after arrival; we do not night-stop on these.

139. "Dry stores" refers to dry food like biscuits, instant noodles etc.

140. Low-cost carrier terminal.

141. The distribution of in-flight entertainment is only relevant on certain airlines like AirAsia X, where passengers are required to pay extra for the device.

142. Turnaround is the time the aircraft spends on the ground between landing and the next take-off.

143. The second most populous German state.

144. Malaysian *Mamaks* have Indian Muslim origins. *Mamak* stalls can be found throughout west Malaysia. In Malaysia, hanging out at a *Mamak* stall is practically a culture.

Part Three: Inside the Trading Room

Why Invest?

145. "The Richest Man in the Last Five Thousand Years, the Wealth of Jin Yong Has Become a Legend of Rivers and Lakes (ETC)," *News Beezer*, October 30, 2018, https://newsbeezer.com/taiwaneng/the-richest-man-in-the-last-five-thousand-years-the-wealth-of-jin-yong-has-become-a-legend-of-rivers-and-lakes-etc/.

146. The government has awarded tax incentives in an attempt to encourage the development of renewable energy.

147. Also known as listed companies.

148. That is generated from the business operation.

149. J. B. Maverick, "What Is the Average Annual Return for the S&P 500?" *Investopedia*, https://www.investopedia.com/ask/answers/042415/what-average-annual-return-sp-500.asp.

150. Kathleen Elkins, "Warren Buffet: Most People Shouldn't Pick Single Stocks—Here's How to Invest Instead," *CNBC*, May 22, 2020, https://www.cnbc.com/2020/05/22/warren-buffett-most-people-shouldnt-pick-single-stocks.

151. Gary Smith and Heidi Margaret Artigue, "Another Look at Dollar Cost Averaging," *The Journal of Investing*, 27, no. 2 (2018), DOI: https://doi.org/10.3905/joi.2018.27.2.066.

152. R.B. (Biff) Matthews and Doug McCutcheon, "Compound Interest May Not Be Einstein's Eight Wonder, But It Is a Powerful Tool for Investors," *The Globe and Mail*, November 12, 2019, https://www.theglobeandmail.com/investing/investment-ideas/article-compound-interest-may-not-be-einsteins-eighth-wonder-but-it-is-a/.

153. Which is a huge reason why many people lose money in the stock market.

154. "Good Quarter," *GFI Investment Counsel Ltd.*, 2013, 2013 Summer GoodQuarter.pdf.

155. Such as Standard & Poor's, Moody's and Fitch.

156. "What is a Rating Agency?" *Corporate Finance Institute*, n.d., https://corporatefinanceinstitute.com/resources/knowledge/finance/rating-agency.

157.   Vivek Kaul, "Is Inflation Nullifying Your Pay Hike?" *DNA*, June 19, 2008, https://www.dnaindia.com/business/report-is-inflation-nullifying-your-pay-hike-1172081

158.   "CPI Inflation Calculator," *U.S. Bureau of Labour Statistics*, n.d., https://www.bls.gov/data/inflation_calculator.htm.

159.   Under the Bretton Wood agreement, countries all over the world maintain a fixed exchange rate between their currency and the dollar.

160.   Government bonds.

161.   A.k.a quantitative easing.

162.   Plus stimulate.

163.   "Keynes on Inflation," *Commanding Heights*, n.d., https://www.pbs.org/wgbh/commandingheights/shared/minitext/ess_inflation.html.

164.   Matthew Johnston, "Worst Cases of Hyperinflation in History," *Investopedia*, December 6, 2019, https://www.investopedia.com/articles/personal-finance/122915/worst-hyperinflations-history.asp.

165.   Scott Baldauf, "In Zimbabwe, Bread Costs Z$10 Million," *The Christian Science Monitor*, March 25, 2008, https://www.csmonitor.com/World/Africa.

166.   Matthew Johnston, "Worst Cases of Hyperinflation in History," *Investopedia*, December 6, 2019, https://www.investopedia.com/articles/personal-finance/122915/worst-hyperinflations-history.asp.

167.   Or operating cost.

168.   As a result of the Covid-19 outbreak.

169.   Ben Winck, "We are not out of the woods: Bond King Jeff Gundlach reopens his bets against the stock market as the coronavirus rages," *Business Insider*, April 27, 2020, https://markets.businessinsider.com/news/stocks/bond-king-gundlach-reopens-stock-market-shorts-amid-coronavirus-threat-2020-4-1029134463#.

170.   Also known as risk management.

171.   A company that owns and operates many types of income-producing commercial real estates.

172.   "Sunway Reit," n.d., http://www.sunwayreit.com

173.   James Chen, "Real Estate Investment Trust (REIT)," *Investopedia*, Updated June 30, 2020, https://www.investopedia.com/terms/r/reit.asp.

174.   "Manulife Investment Management," *Manulife*, July 2020, https://www.fundsupermart.com.my/fsmone/admin/buy/factsheet/factsheetMYML007.pdf.

Risk Management

175.   "Road Traffic Injuries," *World Health Organisation*, February 7, 2020, https://www.who.int/news-room/fact-sheets/detail/road-traffic-injuries.

176.   Such as improved technology and the introduction of anti-collision systems.

177.   Such as more stringent traffic rules and enhanced training programmes.

178.   An option to sell assets at an agreed price on or before a particular date.

179. David Dierking, "Benefits of Holding Stocks for the Long Term," *Investopedia*, May 18, 2020, https://www.investopedia.com.

180. Andrea Riquier, "Don't Time the Market, but If You Do, Here's When the Bear Might Come Knocking," *Market Watch*, December 7, 2019, https://www.marketwatch.com.

Asset Allocation

181. That relies on the production and exports of agricultural products and raw materials.

182. Samuel Osborne, "India to Overtake China as Most Populous Country Within a Decade, UN Report Finds," *Independent*, June 22, 2019, https://www.independent.co.uk/news/world/asia.

183. Rick Matthews, "U.S. GDP Is 70 Percent Personal Consumption: Inside the Numbers," *Mic*, September 21, 2012, https://www.mic.com/articles/15097/us-gdp-is-70-percent-personal-consumption-inside-the-numbers.

184. "Emerging Market and Developing Economies Growth," *European Commission*, n.d., https://ec.europa.eu/knowledge4policy/foresight.

185. Charles E. Boyle, "China Wakes Up as the World Watches," *Insurance Journal*, July 19, 2004, https://www.insurancejournal.com/magazines/mag-features/2004/07/19/44587.htm.

186. Mark Buckle, "Black Cat, White Cat…" *China Daily*, Updated August 2, 2018, http://www.chinadaily.com.

187. Abraham Denmark, "40 Years Ago, Deng Xiaoping Changed China—and the World," *Washington Post*, December 19, 2018, https://www.washingtonpost.com/news/monkey-cage.

188. Where prices are determined by market forces.

189. Richard Evans, *Deng Xiaoping and the Making of Modern China*, (Westminster, London: Penguin Books, 1995)

190. Wayne M. Morrison, "China's Economic Rise: History, Trends, Challenges, and Implications for the United States," *Congressional Research Service*, Updated June 25, 2019, https://fas.org/sgp/crs/row/RL33534.pdf.

191. Since the Reform and Opening in 1978 through 2018.

192. Caleb Silver, "The Top 20 Economies in the World," *Investopedia*, https://www.investopedia.com/insights/worlds-top-economies.

193. Amelia Lucas, "Starbucks Reopens China Cafes After Temporary Closures Due to Coronavirus," *CNBC*, https://www.cnbc.com/2020/02/27/.

194. Jonathan Ponciano, "The Countries With the Most Billionaires," *Forbes*, 2020, https://www.forbes.com/sites/jonathanponciano/2020/04/08/the-countries-with-the-most-billionaires-in-2020.

195. Zhuang Qiange, "129 Chinese Firms On Fortune Global 500," *China Daily*, Updated July 22, 2019, https://www.chinadaily.com.cn.

196. Elaine Chan and Sidney Leng, "Hong Kong Economy Surpassed by Neighbour Shenzhen for First Time in 2018 as China's High-Tech Hub Soars," *South China Morning Post*, February 27, 2019, https://www.scmp.com/economy/china-economy.

197. Ray Dalio, "Work Principle 5; Believability Weight Your Decision Making," *Linkedin*, February 7, 2019, https://www.linkedin.com/pulse/work-principle-5-believability-weight-your-decision-making-ray-dalio.

198. Elaine Chan and Sidney Leng, "Hong Kong Economy Surpassed by Neighbour Shenzhen for First Time in 2018 as China's High-Tech Hub Soars," *South China Morning Post*, February 27, 2019, https://www.scmp.com/economy/china-economy.

199. Roy Katayama and Divyanshi Wadhwa, "Half of the World's Poor Live in Just 5 Countries," *World Bank*, January 9, 2019, https://blogs.worldbank.org/opendata/half-world-s-poor-live-just-5-countries.

200. "The World Bank in China," n.d., https://www.worldbank.org/en/country/china/overview.

201. Lingyu, "Chinese University Graduates Rise Exponentially, Have Diverse Career Options," *Xinhua Net*, June 24, 2019, http://www.xinhuanet.com/english/2019-06/24/c_138169311.htm.

202. Rebecca Fannin, "A Look at China Beating the U.S. on Patents Can Be Misleading," *Forbes*, October 20, 2019, https://www.forbes.com/sites/rebeccafannin/2019/10/20/a-look-at-china-beating-the-us-on-patents-can-be-misleading.

203. WIPO is an agency of the United Nations (UN) for intellectual property services, policy, information and cooperation.

204. Geneva, "China Becomes Top Filer of International Patents in 2019 Amid Robust Growth for WIPO's IP Services, Treaties and Finances," *WIPO*, April 7, 2020, https://www.wipo.int/pressroom/en/articles/2020.

205. Akito Tanaka, "China in Pole Position for 5G Era With a Third of Key Patents," *Nikkei Asian Review*, May 3, 2019, https://asia.nikkei.com/Spotlight/5G-networks.

206. Karen Campbell et al., "The 5G Economy," *IHS Markit*, November 2019, https://www.qualcomm.com/media/documents/files/ihs-5g-economic-impact-study-2019.pdf.

207. Thomas Colson, "RANKED: These Will Be the 21 Most Powerful Economies in 2030," *Business Insider*, August 31, 2017, https://www.businessinsider.com/pwc-predicts-the-most-powerful-economies-by-2030-2017-8.

208. An intergovernmental organisation that fosters and promotes economic development and prosperity through cooperation of its member countries.

209. "GDP Long-Term Forecast," *OECD*, n.d., https://data.oecd.org/gdp/gdp-long-term-forecast.htm.

210. "Buffet Indicator: China Stock Market Valuations and Expected Future Returns," *Guru Focus*, September 4, 2020, https://www.gurufocus.com.

211. "Total Market Value of U.S. Stock Market," n.d., https://siblisresearch.com/data/us-stock-market-value/.

212. Caleb Silver, "The Top 20 Economies in the World," *Investopedia*, https://www.investopedia.com/insights/worlds-top-economies.

213. "Buffet Indicator: Strongly Overvalued," *Current Market Valuation*, Updated September 17, 2020, http://www.currentmarketvaluation.com/models/buffet-indicator.php.

214. Elvis Picardo, "10 Countries With the Biggest Forex Reserves," *Investopedia*, March 7, 2020, https://www.investopedia.com/articles/investing/033115/10-countries-biggest-forex-reserves.asp.

215. "World Population Prospects 2019," *United Nations*, 2019, https://un.org/development/desa/pd/

216. "China's Two-Child Policy Results in Largest Number of Newborns Since 2000: Official," *Xinhuanet*, March 11, 2017, http://xinhuanet.com.

217. "Made in China 2025," *Institute for Security & Development Policy*, June 2018, https://isdp.eu/publication/made-china-2025/.

218. Lan Suying, "New Plan Announced to Boost China's 'Go West' Strategy," *NBD*, January 17, 2017, http://www.nbdpress.com/articles/2017-01-17/964.html.

219. Robert A. Rohde and Richard A. Muller, "Air Pollution in China: Mapping of Concentrations and Sources," n.d., http://berkeleyearth.org.

220. Bonnie West, "Chinese Coal-Fired Electricity Generation Expected to Flatten as Mix Shifts to Renewables," *U.S. Energy Information Administration*, September 29, 2017, https://www.eia.gov.

221. "China Consumes Nearly as Much Coal as the Rest of the World Combines," *U.S. Energy Information Administration*, January 29, 2013, https://eia.gov.

222. Echo Xie, "China Tech Giants Wake Up to Renewable Energy, but Fossil Fuels Still Dominate as Electricity Source," *South China Morning Post*, January 11, 2020, https://www.scmp.com

223. By shutting down polluting mills and factories.

224. Andriy Blokhin, "The 5 Countries That Produce the Most Carbon Dioxide (CO2)," *Investopedia*, November 14, 2019, http://investopedia.com.

225. Excluding large hydro.

226. Cayo Ajadi et al., "Global Trends in Renewable Energy Investment," *Frankfurt School*, 2020, https://www.fs-unep-centre.org/wp-content/uploads/2020/06/GTR_2020.pdf, 43.

227. Andrew Winston, "China Leads the Clean Economy Race," *Harvard Business Review*, September 23, 2010, https://hbr.org/2010/09/china-leads-clean-economy.

228. Sumit Chakrabarti, "Solar Power Statistics in China 2019," *Solar Feeds*, August 22, 2019, https://solarfeeds.com/solar-power-statistics-in-china.

229. Eva Botkin-Kowacki, "China's Forest Conservation Program Shows Proof of Success," *The Christian Science Monitor*, March 19, 2016, https://www.csmonitor.com/Science/2016/0319/China-s-forest-conservation-program-shows-proof-of-success.

230. "Belt and Road Initiative," *The World Bank*, March 29, 2018, https://www.worldbank.org/en/topic/regional-integration/brief/belt-and-road-initiative.

231. When converted into local currencies.

232. The *Soros Fund Management* bankrupted the Bank of England in 1992 by shorting the British pound.

233. Heather Bell, "Jim Rogers on the Next 10 Years," *Seeking Alpha*, October 11, 2009, https://seekingalpha.com/article/165918-jim-rogers-on-the-next-10-years.

234. Angus Maddison, "The Interaction Between Asia and the West, 1500-2003," *Contours of the World Economy 1-2030 A.D.*, (Oxford: Oxford University Press, 2007).

235. "Indian Population," *Worldometer*, https://www.worldometers.info/world-population/india-population/.

236. "India 2019," *Population Pyramid*, 2019, https://www.populationpyramid.net/india/2019/.

237. "China's Birth Rate Is Now Almost Half That of India's," *Times of India*, January 23, 2020, https://timesofindia.indiatimes.com/india/chinas-birth-rate-is-now-almost-half-that-of-ind ias/articleshow/73552739.cms.

238. "China's Birth Rate Is Now Almost Half That of India's," *Times of India*, January 23, 2020, https://timesofindia.indiatimes.com/india/chinas-birth-rate-is-now-almost-half-that-of-ind ias/articleshow/73552739.cms.

239. "Japan Fertility Rate Drops to the Lowest Level In 12 Years," *Nikkei Asian Review*, June 5, 2020, https://asia.nikkei.com/Economy/Japan-fertility-rate-drops-to-the-lowest-level-in-12-year s.

240. Jaideep Shenoy, "India's Labour Force Will Expand to 170 Million by 2020: Assocham," *The Times of India*, January 19, 2017, https://timesofindia.com.

241. Saikat Pyne, "Exclusive: The 'Father of Pentium Processor' Vinod Dham Talks About Startups and Where India is Headed," *Business Insider India*, https://www.businessinsider.in/exclusive-the-father-of-pentiumprocessor-vinod-dham-tal ks-about-startups-and-where-india-is-headed/articleshow/50932473.cms.

242. Caleb Silver, "The Top 20 Economies in the World," *Investopedia*, https://www.investopedia.com/insights/worlds-top-economies.

243. "India Real GDP Growth," *CEIC*, 2020, https://www.ceicdata.com/en/indicator/india/real-gdp-growth.

244. Ians, "India Added 1,300 Startups Including 7 Unicorns in 2019," *The News Minute*, November 7, 2019, https://www.thenewsminute.com.

245. "India to Have 100,000 Startups by 2025: Mohandes Pai at NSE Tech Conclave," *Business Standard*, February 27, 2018, https://business-standard.com.

246. Remya Lakshmanan, "Service Sector in India: A Paradigm Shift," *Invest India*, May 16, 2019, https://investindia.gov.in.

247. Hemant Singh, "Composition and Contribution of Service Sector in India," *Jagran Josh*, n.d., https://jagranjosh.com.

248. "India Insight: $ 10 Trillion GDP by 2030? Not Quite, but Almost," *Bloomberg*, October 2, 2019, https://bloomberg.com.

249. "IMF Says India's Real Interest Rates Will Fall 150 Bps Between 2020 and 2030," *Money Control*, August 2, 2018, https://moneycontrol.com.

250. Abheek Singhi, Nimisha Jain and Kanika Sanghi, "The New Indian: The Many Facets of a Changing Consumer," *BCG*, March 20, 2017, https://bcg.com.

251. "The Long View: How Will the Global Economic Order Change by 2050?" *The World in 2050—Summary Report*, February 2017, https://www.pwc.com.

252. John E. Marthinsen, "India's Demonetisation: What Were They Thinking?" *Babson College*, April 2017, https://babson.edu.

253. "Withdrawal of Legal Tender Status for Rs 500 and Rs 1,000 Notes: RBI Notice," *Reserve Bank of India*, November 8, 2016, https://rbi.org.in.

254. Aishwarya Krishnan, "Demonetisation Anniversary: Decoding the Effects of Indian Currency Notes Ban," *The Economic Times*, Updated May 21, 2019, https://economictimes.indiatimes.com.

255. Utpal Bhaskar, "26.02 Million Households Get Electricity Connections Under Saubhagya Scheme," *Live Mint*, Updated March 31 , 2019, https://livemint.com.

256. Via efficient resource allocation.

257. "Census of India: Language," 2011, https://censusindia.gov.in/2011Census/C-16_25062018_NEW.pdf.

258. "Make in India: The Vision, New Processes, Sectors, Infrastructure and Mindset," *Make in India*, n.d., https://makeinindia.com.

259. Chris Owens, "The 11 Biggest Blackouts of All Time," *The Blackout Report*, July 5, 2019, https://theblackoutreport.co.uk/2019/07/05/11-biggest-blackouts.

260. Sujay Mehdudia and Smriti Kak Ramachandran, "Worst Outage Cripples North India," *The Hindu*, Updated July 5, 2016, https://thehindu.com.

261. Anjali Jaiswal, "Transitioning India's Economy to Clean Energy," *NRDC*, November 5, 2019, https://nrdc.org/experts/anjali-jaiswal/transitioning-indias-economy-clean-energy.

262. Sagar Parikh, "Tata EVision Fully Electric Concept Unveiled in Geneva," *India Autos Blog*, March 7, 2018, https://indianautosblog.com.

263. "Bloodbath on Dalal Street Erodes Nearly Rs 5 Lakh Cr Investor Wealth," *Republic World*, Updated February 28, 2020, https://republicworld.com/india-news.

264. Caleb Silver, "The Top 20 Economies in the World," *Investopedia*, https://investopedia.com/insights/worlds-top-economies.

265. K. Natwar Singh, "What India Taught Max Muller," *The Tribune*, May 20, 2018, https://tribuneindia.com.

266. "Establishment," *ASEAN*, n.d., https://asean.org/asean/about-asean/overview/.

267. "ASEAN Key Figures 2019," *ASEAN Stats*, 2019, https://aseanstats.org/wp-content/uploads/2019/11/ASEAN_Key_Figures_2019.pdf.

268. Jack Myint, "What is ASEAN," *US-ASEAN*, Updated October 24, 2019, https://usasean.org/why-asean/what-is-asean.

269. "ASEA Key Figures 2019," *ASEAN*, 2019, https://aseanstats.org/wp-content/uploads/2019/11/ASEAN_Key_Figures_2019.pdf.

270. "ASEAN Growth Slower Than Forecasted," *The ASEAN Post*, December 30, 2019, https://theaseanpost.com/article/asean-growth-slower-forecasted.

271. Erin Duffin, "Real GDP Growth of the United States from 1990 to 2019," February 3, 2020, https://statista.com/statistics/188165/annual-gdp-growth-of-the-united-states-since-1990/.

272. Kwong Mook Shian et al., "ASEAN Economic Progress: Prospects," *CARI*, October 23, 2019, www.cariasean.org.

273. The 3 most dynamic and vibrant ASEAN economies.

274. "ASEAN Growth Slower than Forecasted," *The ASEAN Post*, December 30, 2019, https://theaseanpost.com/article/asean-growth-slower-forecasted.

275. "The World Bank in Vietnam," *World Bank*, Updated April 27, 2020, https://www.worldbank.org/en/country/vietnam/overview.

276. An American political journalism company based in Virginia.

277. Jasmine Le, "Politico: Vietnam the World's No. 1 Country in Covid-19 Fight," *Vietnam Times*, May 23, 2020, https://vietnamtimes.org.vn.
278. "Cambodia Population," *Worldometer*, 2020, https://www.worldometers.info.
279. "The World Bank in Cambodia," *World Bank*, April 17, 2020, https://www.worldbank.org.
280. "Indonesia Population," *Worldometer*, 2020, https://www.worldometers.info.
280. "ASEAN - Association of Southeast Asian Nations," *Country Economy*, n.d., https://countryeconomy.com/countries.groups/asean.
281. Ibid.
282. Jeff Desjardins, "Chart: The World's Largest 10 Economies in 2030," *Visual Capitalist*, January 11, 2019, https://www.visualcapitalist.com/worlds-largest-10-economies-2030/.
283. "Facts & Figures," *Embassy of the Republic of Indonesia*, n.d., https://www.embassyofindonesia.org.
284. "Philippines Population," *Worldometer*, 2020, https://www.worldometers.info.
285. "ASEAN - Association of Southeast Asian Nations," *Country Economy*, n.d., https://countryeconomy.com/countries.groups/asean.
286. "About the Philippines," *Gov.Ph.,* n.d., https://www.gov.ph/about-the-philippines.
287. "Brunei Population," *Worldometer*, 2020, https://www.worldometers.info.
288. "Thailand Population," *Worldometer*, 2020, https://www.worldometers.info.
289. "ASEAN - Association of Southeast Asian Nations," *Country Economy*, n.d., https://countryeconomy.com/countries.groups/asean.
290. "Total Value of Tourism's Contribution to the Gross Domestic Product in Thailand From 2017 to First Quarter of 2020, *Statista*, n.d., https://www.statista.com.
291. John Le Fevre, "Thailand Morning News for June 30," *AEC News Today*, June 30, 2020, https://aecnewstoday.com/2020/thailand-morning-news-for-june-30-2/.
292. "Laos Population," *Worldometer*, 2020, https://www.worldometers.info.
293. "ASEAN - Association of Southeast Asian Nations," *Country Economy*, n.d., https://countryeconomy.com/countries.groups/asean.
294. "Myanmar Population," *Worldometer*, 2020, https://www.worldometers.info.
295. "ASEAN - Association of Southeast Asian Nations," *Country Economy*, n.d., https://countryeconomy.com/countries.groups/asean.
296. "Singapore Population," *Worldometer*, 2020, https://www.worldometers.info.
297. "ASEAN - Association of Southeast Asian Nations," *Country Economy*, n.d., https://countryeconomy.com/countries.groups/asean.
298. Ibid.
299. Dan Steinbock, "The Rise and Decline of Four Little Dragons," *Asia One*, March 11, 2017, https://www.asiaone.com/business/rise-and-decline-four-little-dragons.
300. "Malaysia Population," *Worldometer*, 2020, https://www.worldometers.info.
301. "ASEAN - Association of Southeast Asian Nations," *Country Economy*, n.d., https://countryeconomy.com/countries.groups/asean.
302. "Malaysia GDP Growth Rate 1961-2020," *Macrotrends*, n.d., https://www.macrotrends.net/countries/MYS/malaysia/gdp-growth-rate.
303. "The World in 2050," *PWC*, February 2017, https://www.pwc.com/gx/en/issues/economy/the-world-in-2050.html.